LEARN to LISTEN
LISTEN to LEARN

Academic Listening and Note-Taking

Second Edition

Longman

Roni S. Lebauer

Learn to Listen; Listen to Learn, Second Edition

Pearson Education, 10 Bank Street, White Plains, NY 10606

Editorial director: Allen Ascher
Executive editor: Louisa Hellegers
Development editor: Lise Minovitz
Director of design and production: Rhea Banker
Associate director of electronic production: Aliza Greenblatt
Managing editor: Linda Moser
Production manager: Ray Keating
Production editor: Martin Yu
Associate technical production manager: Steven D. Greydanus
Senior manufacturing manager: Patrice Fraccio
Manufacturing supervisor: Edith Pullman
Photo research: Diana Nott
Cover design: Carey Davies
Cover photo: Scott Cunningham
Interior design: Steven D. Greydanus
Credits: See pages xiii–xiv.

Library of Congress Cataloging-in-Publication Data

Lebauer, Roni S.
    Learn to listen; listen to learn: academic listening and note-
taking / Roni S. Lebauer.—2nd ed.
        p.   cm.
    Includes bibliographical references and indexes.
    ISBN: 0-13-919432-0 (alk. paper)
    1. Lecture method in teaching.   2. Listening.   3. Note-taking.
4. English language—Study and teaching—United States—
Foreign speakers.   I. Title.

LB2393.L43   2000
371.39'6—dc21   99-047758
                                                        CIP

9 10—PHX—05

CONTENTS

PREFACE

▣ Overview

This book is designed to help advanced ESL/EFL students prepare for the demands of academic lecture comprehension and note-taking.

Listening to lectures and taking notes involves more than language skills alone. Rather, lecture comprehension and note-taking require skills in *evaluating information* (deciding what is important and needs to be noted), *organizing information* (seeing how ideas relate to each other), and *predicting information* (anticipating the content and direction of a lecture). This book teaches these skills and also includes exercises focusing on the acquisition of vocabulary and the recognition of language cues (lexical, grammatical, and paralinguistic cues) that are used in lectures to signal lecture organization.

The goal of this book is to teach students *how* to listen to a lecture and take notes: how to recognize lecture organization, use lecture cues and conventions that indicate organization and emphasis, recognize redundancy, and predict information. The text teaches these skills and provides numerous opportunities to practice them.

Another goal of this book is to provide materials that replicate the style and function of academic lectures. The lectures in the text have been selected to motivate students to listen, not just to complete a language task but also to gain knowledge about a variety of topics. To achieve this goal, a diversity of lectures allow teachers to choose topics based on students' interests and needs. These lectures cover a wide range of fields, and are accessible to the layperson yet still of interest to the specialist. The text also aims to simulate the lecture situation by allowing teachers to either deliver the lectures live (using the outlines in the Teacher's Manual), use taped lectures given by a variety of speakers, or both. In addition, many activities in the book include lecture excerpts originally given to audiences comprising native English speakers.

The text is divided into seven units. Units 1 through 5 focus on the skills necessary to comprehend and take notes on lectures. Unit 1, "Pre-Coursework Evaluation," contains lectures and exercises that help the teacher evaluate students' levels prior to using this book. The lecture in this section is about the process of lecture comprehension, and thus it informs as well as tests. Unit 2, "Looking at Lecture Transcripts," contains lecture transcripts and exercises designed to help students become more aware of lecture discourse style, such as the high degree of paraphrase and redundancy in lectures and the use of cues to introduce topics, signal organization, and conclude lectures. Unit 3, "Note-Taking Basics," contains guidelines, information, and exercises on note-taking basics: noting key words, using symbols, and using space on the page to show relationships between ideas. Unit 4, "Noting Numbers and Statistics," contains lectures and exercises on noting numbers, years, and statistics. Unit 5, "Listening for Organization in Lectures," introduces students to different organizational plans used in lectures. The students then practice comprehending, predicting, and taking notes from lecture excerpts that demonstrate these organizational plans. (Exercise material in this unit comes directly from transcripts of college lectures given to native English speakers.)

Unit 6, "Lecture Comprehension and Note-Taking Practice," provides holistic practice of the skills taught in Units 1 through 5. This unit contains twelve lectures, with activities generally occurring in the following sequence:

- *Pre-Lecture Discussion.* This activity provides background information, elicits interest, and provides a vehicle for the introduction of relevant vocabulary. The discussion often revolves around readings related to the topic.

- *Preparing for the Lecture.* Students discuss their expectations of the lecture based on the lecture title and the Pre-Lecture Discussion. This helps students build up additional background knowledge. It also helps them make predictions about lecture content and organization before listening.

- *Listening for the Larger Picture.* Students listen to the lecture once without taking notes and then answer questions. This helps them focus on getting the larger picture without becoming preoccupied with details.

- *Organization.* Students read a summary of the lecture organization to affirm their initial comprehension or guide them toward better comprehension.

- *Defining Vocabulary.* Students listen to vocabulary from the lecture in different contexts and choose the correct meaning.

- *Note-Taking Practice.* Students listen to the lecture a second time and take notes. Minimal comments in the margin guide the students by giving information about the lecture organization, while at the same time allowing them to develop their own note-taking style. After that, they revise or rewrite their notes so that they are better organized and include all relevant information.

- *Post-Lecture Discussion.* Students participate in group discussions that encourage communication about issues raised in the lecture. Often these discussions involve additional related readings.

- *Using Your Notes.* Students test the accuracy of their notes by using them to answer questions representative of those on university tests, such as True/False, multiple-choice, short-answer, and essay questions.

- *Comparing Ideas.* Students compare and discuss their notes to discover alternative and perhaps more effective ways to take notes.

- *Using Vocabulary.* Students check their comprehension by listening to new vocabulary in different contexts and choosing the best paraphrase.

- *Retaining Vocabulary.* Students choose words from the chapter that they want to remember. Since all vocabulary is not equally important to all students, students take responsibility for learning the vocabulary that is relevant to them.

- *Speaking and Listening Activity* or *Writing Activity.* Students use information from the lecture and related reading(s) in an extension Speaking and Listening Activity, such as a presentation or debate, or Writing Activity, such as an essay or letter.

Unit 7, "Post-Coursework Evaluation," contains two lectures that can serve as a final evaluation. Students are given less guidance and preparation for listening and note-taking, and they can use their notes as they might in a university situation. That is, they put them aside and use them as a reference in preparation for a quiz one or two weeks later.

Audiocassettes and a Teacher's Manual accompany this text. The Teacher's Manual contains teaching suggestions, lecture outlines, lecture transcripts, exercise transcripts, and answer keys. It also has quizzes for the lectures in Unit 7. The tapes provide exposure to a variety of speaking styles and can be a valuable resource for work in class or the language laboratory.

▣ Guidelines for Presenting Lectures

This book has been designed for maximum flexibility. Depending on the needs and expectations of their students, teachers have two options for presenting lectures. One option is to use the audiocassettes, which allow teachers to expose students to a number of speaking styles and accents. Another option is for teachers to present live lectures to the class. To assist teachers in presenting lectures naturally, lecture outlines are included in the Teacher's Manual. The outlines give the basic information and structure of the lectures; it is up to the teacher to paraphrase, repeat, add information, go off on tangents, and summarize as necessary. The Teacher's Manual also includes transcripts of the audiotaped lectures to show how the lectures could sound when presented.

Live delivery of the lectures by ESL/EFL teachers cannot, of course, be completely authentic. Research has shown that ESL/EFL teachers adapt their language to fit the level of their nonnative speaker audiences. Although it may be impossible to completely erase all such "teacher talk" from lecture delivery, teachers should be aware of whether and how much they adapt their language. The goal should be to help students listen to lectures as they would be presented to native speaker listeners. Therefore, teachers should aim for their usual rate of speaking, vocabulary, and amount of repetition and paraphrase.

▣ Guidelines for Sequencing Material

The material in this book does not need to be followed sequentially. Rather, it allows the teachers to plan courses according to the needs and interests of each class. The chart below gives some general guidelines about sequencing.

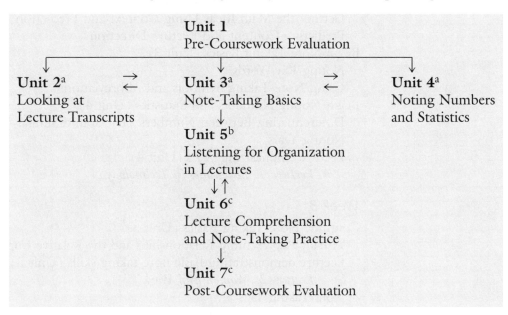

Unit 1
Pre-Coursework Evaluation

Unit 2ᵃ
Looking at
Lecture Transcripts

Unit 3ᵃ
Note-Taking Basics

Unit 4ᵃ
Noting Numbers
and Statistics

Unit 5ᵇ
Listening for Organization
in Lectures

Unit 6ᶜ
Lecture Comprehension
and Note-Taking Practice

Unit 7ᶜ
Post-Coursework Evaluation

ᵃ Material in Units 2, 3, and 4 can be presented simultaneously in order to vary activities and skills practice.

ᵇ Unit 5 does not have to be covered completely or in sequence before going on to Unit 6. Rather, a teacher might choose to cover one or two organizational plans in Unit 5 and then choose a lecture in Unit 6 that uses the organizational plans. (Appendix A contains an index of lectures organized according to organizational plan.)

ᶜ Units 6 and 7 contain numerous lectures that can be done in any order. However, the lectures and exercises toward the beginning of the sections are generally easier than those toward the end of the sections.

⊞ Example Syllabi

The following syllabi show how the textbook can be used for different courses: a single course devoted primarily to lecture comprehension and note-taking or multi-skill courses with a lecture comprehension and note-taking component.

EXAMPLE SYLLABUS FOR A LECTURE COMPREHENSION AND NOTE-TAKING COURSE

Some programs offer courses that focus on lecture comprehension and note-taking. The following syllabus shows one way that the textbook can be used for a thirty-hour course, three hours per week.

Week 1
Syllabus
Pre-Coursework Evaluation (Unit 1)
Begin Looking at Lecture Transcripts (Unit 2)
   Comparing the Language of Lecturing to the Language of Writing
   Recognizing Cues
   Recognizing Paraphrase, Repetition, Exemplification, and Tangential
      Information
   Summarizing Key Differences between the Language of Lecturing and the
      Language of Writing

Week 2
Continue Looking at Lecture Transcripts (Unit 2)
   Getting the Main Ideas Using Context and Prediction
   Predicting Content and Lecture Direction
Begin Note-Taking Basics (Unit 3)
   Noting Key Words
   Using Note-Taking Symbols and Abbreviations
Begin Noting Numbers and Statistics (Unit 4)
   Differentiating Between Numbers That Sound Similar
   Noting Years
   Lecture emphasizing years (Unit 4)
      Lecture 4: Milestones in Technology

Week 3
Continue Note-Taking Basics (Unit 3)
   Visually Representing Relationships and the Relative Importance of Information
   Lecture demonstrating basic note-taking skills (Unit 3)
      Lecture 2: Women and Work
   Note-Taking Tips
Begin Listening for Organization in Lectures (Unit 5)
   Recognizing Introductions and Conclusions
Begin Organizational Plans Within Lectures (Unit 5)
   Defining a Term
   Listing Subtopics
   Lecture using definitions and lists (Unit 6)
      Lecture 6: How to Deal with Stress **or**
      Lecture 9: Amnesty International

Week 4

Continue Organizational Plans Within Lectures (Unit 5)
  Describing a Causal Relationship
  Exemplying a Topic
  Lecture describing a causal relationship and exemplifying a topic (Unit 6)
     Lecture 7: Acid Rain
Continue Noting Numbers and Statistics (Unit 4)
  Noting Large Numbers in Isolation
  Noting Fractions and Decimals

Week 5

Lecture emphasizing dates and larger numbers, fractions, and decimals (Unit 4)
     Lecture 3: American Attitudes toward Work **or**
     Lecture 5: Immigration to the United States
Continue Organizational Plans Within Lectures (Unit 5)
  Describing a Process or Sequence of Events
  Lecture including a description of a process or sequence of events (Unit 6)
     Lecture 8: Archaeological Dating Methods **or**
     Lecture 15: Paging Robodoc: Robots in Medicine

Week 6

Midterm exam
Continue Organizational Plans Within Lectures (Unit 5)
  Classifying Subtopics

Week 7

Continue Organizational Plans Within Lectures (Unit 5)
  Describing characteristics
  Lecture emphasizing or incorporating descriptions and/or classifications (Unit 6)
     Lecture 10: Pheromones
     Lecture 11: The Near Side of the Moon **or**
     Lecture 14: How to Look at Art

Week 8

Continue Organizational Plans Within Lectures (Unit 5)
  Comparing and Contrasting
  Lecture emphasizing comparison and contrast (Unit 6)
     Lecture 13: Voter Turnout in the United States **or**
     Lecture 17: Hall's Classification of Cultures
Tangents (Unit 5)

Week 9

Continue Organizational Plans Within Lectures (Unit 5)
  Making a Generalization and Providing Evidence
  Lecture emphasizing a generalization supported by evidence (Unit 6)
     Lecture 12: Drink Your Green Tea! **or**
     Lecture 16: Earthquakes: Can They Be Predicted?

Week 10

Post-Coursework Evaluation (Unit 7)
     Lecture 18: The Pyramids of Egypt: An Engineering Feat **or**
     Lecture 19: Perfectionism
Final exam based on either of these lectures with retention tests using notes

EXAMPLE SYLLABUS FOR TWO MULTI-SKILL COURSES WITH A LECTURE COMPREHENSION AND NOTE-TAKING COMPONENT

Many programs do not offer separate courses in lecture comprehension; rather, they have a listening and note-taking component in their general curriculum. The following syllabus shows one way that the textbook can be divided over two levels.

Level 1

Pre-Coursework Evaluation (Unit 1)
Looking at Lecture Transcripts (Unit 2)
Note-Taking Basics (Unit 3)
Noting Numbers and Statistics (Unit 4)
    Lecture emphasizing dates and numbers (Unit 4)
        Lecture 3: American Attitudes toward Work **or**
        Lecture 4: Milestones in Technology
Listening for Organization in Lectures (Unit 5)
    Using Introductions to Recognize Lecture Focus and Direction
    Recognizing and Comprehending Conclusions
Begin Organizational Plans Within Lectures
    Defining a Term
    Listing Subtopics
    Describing a Causal Relationship
    Exemplifying a Topic
    Describing a Process or Sequence of Events
    Lectures selected from the following (Unit 6)
        Lecture 6: How to Deal with Stress
        Lecture 7: Acid Rain
        Lecture 8: Archaeological Dating Methods
        Lecture 9: Amnesty International

Level 2

Review of Level 1 material
        Lecture 5: Immigration to the United States (noting large numbers and years)
        Lecture 15: Paging Robodoc: Robots in Medicine (which includes definitions, exemplification, and a description of a process)
Continue Listening for Organization in Lectures (Unit 5)
    Classifying Subtopics
    Describing Characteristics
    Comparing and Contrasting
    Making a Generalization and Providing Evidence
Tangents (Unit 5)
    Lectures selected from the following (Unit 6)
        Lecture 10: Pheromones
        Lecture 11: The Near Side of the Moon
        Lecture 12: Drink Your Green Tea!
        Lecture 13: Voter Turnout in the United States
        Lecture 14: How to Look at Art
        Lecture 16: Earthquakes: Can They Be Predicted?
        Lecture 17: Hall's Classification of Cultures
    Lectures selected from the following (Unit 7)
        Lecture 18: The Pyramids of Egypt: An Engineering Feat **or**
        Lecture 19: Perfectionism

⌘ Key Changes in the Second Edition

Unit 2 has been slightly abridged and adapted. Lectures have been updated and new lectures have been added. Lecture topics continue to reflect a diversity of disciplines, including the arts, humanities, sciences, engineering, computer science, technology, and social sciences. New note-taking activities have been added to Unit 3. Readings have been added to most lecture units to increase students' background knowledge and provide opportunities to see and use relevant vocabulary. Post-lecture comprehension checks have been revised and reflect a range of questions typical of university tests (e.g., True/False, multiple-choice, short-answer, or essay questions). Post-lecture speaking and listening and writing activities have been added to provide opportunities to personalize and expand upon ideas raised in the lectures.

ACKNOWLEDGMENTS

Several people have helped me bring this book to its present form, and each of them deserves my sincere thanks:

- Miho Steinberg and Richard Day for first giving me release time from teaching duties in order to develop materials for an advanced ESL listening comprehension course;

- Ted Plaister and David Rickard for their encouragement of my work in listening comprehension and for providing technical resources and ideas that, way back then, provided stimuli for the first edition of this book;

- Ellen Broidy and the many other professors and speakers whose lectures I transcribed and used to examine lecture discourse and create many of the exercises in this book;

- Leann Stone and Susan Tucker for making sure that my constant audio-tape equipment needs were handled efficiently and with a smile;

- Robin Scarcella and Vicki Bergman-Lanier for providing me with opportunities to pilot my materials in their programs;

- The teachers who took extra time from their usually busy schedules to test these materials and provide feedback: Aaron Albright, Martha Compton, Janice Jensen, Lorraine Kumpf, Wendy Maccoun, Susan Stern, Judy Tanka, Judy Via, and Angeliki Volksman;

- "The Talent" for graciously giving their time and energy in order to help me produce the audiocassettes that accompanied the first edition of this book: Aaron Albright, Jan Barber, Chris Bellerive, Ellen Broidy, Greg Conner, Jane DeSelm, Gordon Johnson, Lorraine Kumpf, Gary Rodrigue, and Michelle Ryan;

- The editorial and production teams at Prentice-Hall and Pearson Education for their enthusiasm, talent, and professionalism: Brenda White, Jan Stephan, Martha Masterson, Nancy Baxer, Sheryl Olinsky Borg, Louisa Hellegers, Lise Minovitz (editor *extraordinaire*), Diana Nott, Marianne Carello, and Martin Yu;

- The many anonymous reviewers whose thoughtful comments helped me revise and revise and revise; and

- Michelle Rene-Ryan for being herself and being part of my life.

Roni S. Lebauer

CREDITS

⧉ Text

Unit 2, Lecture 2: J. Greenberg, "Mental Health of Working Women," *Science News*, 117 (April 26, 1980), p. 266. **Unit 4, Lecture 3:** Christopher Caggiano, "What Do Workers Want?" *Inc.* (November 1992), pp. 101–102. **Unit 4, Lecture 4:** *American Heritage Dictionary Second College Edition,* Houghton Mifflin Company, Boston, MA, 1982; Sharon Begly with B. J. Sigesmund, "The Houses of Invention," *Newsweek* (Winter Extra 1997–1998), © 1997, Newsweek, Inc. All rights reserved. Reprinted by permission; *The Universal Almanac, 1997,* John W. Wright (Ed.), Andrews and McMeel, A Universal Press Syndicate Co., Kansas City, MO, 1996, pp. 591–593; Michio Kaku, "As Science Finds Answers, It Uncovers Questions," *Los Angeles Times* (March 12, 1998), p. B-2. **Unit 4, Lecture 5:** Emma Lazarus, "The New Colossus." **Unit 5:** Ellen Broidy, UC Irvine Research Librarian; Andrew Harper, "Academic Listening Comprehension: Does the Sum of the Parts Make Up the Whole?" Occasional Paper #7. Dept. of ESL., University of Hawaii at Manoa (1985); Michael Rost "On-line Summaries as Representations of Lecture Understanding" (1994), in John Flowerdew (Ed.) *Academic Listening: Research Perspectives,* Cambridge University Press, Cambridge, England: pp. 93–127. **Unit 6, Lecture 6:** Tom Greening and Dick Hobson, *Instant Relief: The Encyclopedia of Self-Help,* Simon and Schuster Pub., New York, 1979, pp. 329–352; T. H. Holmes and R. H. Rahe, "The Social Readjustment Rating Scale" (1967), reprinted from *Journal of Psychosomatic Research*, Vol. 11, with permission from Elsevier Science. **Unit 6, Lecture 7:** E. J. Kormandy, *Concepts of Ecology, 3rd ed.*, Prentice Hall Inc., Englewood Cliffs, NJ, 1984, pp. 274–277; Anne LaBastille, "The International Acid Test," *Sierra* (May/June 1986), p. 51. Reprinted with permission of Sierra; Bernard J. Nebel and Richard T. Wright, *The Way the World Works: Environmental Science*, 5th ed., Prentice Hall Inc., Upper Saddle River, NJ, 1996, pp. 382–385; 400–408. **Unit 6, Lecture 8:** Judith Crosher, *Ancient Egypt,* Penguin Group, New York, 1993; Dina Ingber, "New Tools Unearth the Past," *Science Digest* (Nov–Dec. 1980), pp. 99–101; Anne Millard, *Pyramids,* Larousse Kingfisher Chambers Inc., New York, 1996; "Project 1: Dinosaur Footprints" and "Project 2: Search for Neanderthals" are sponsored by the nonprofit Earthwatch Institute, www.earthwatch.org. **Unit 6, Lecture 9:** Poem is one of many versions of Pastor Martin Niemoller's words that appeared in the *Congressional Record*, Oct. 14, 1968, p. 31636. **Unit 6, Lecture 10:** Gwenda Blair, "Researchers Sniff Out Pheromones," *Los Angeles Times* (Dec. 29, 1997), pp. S1, S4. Copyright © 1997 *LA Times*. Reprinted by permission; H. H. Shorey, *Animal Communication by Pheromones*, Academic Press, New York, NY, 1976. **Unit 6, Lecture 11:** Susan Carpenter, "Gearing Up for the New Race to Space," *Los Angeles Times* (June 23, 1998), pp. E1, E5; K. C. Cole, "Water Possibly Found on Moon," *Los Angeles Times* (March 6, 1998), pp. A1, A18; Robert T. Dixon, *Dynamic Astronomy*, Prentice Hall Inc., Englewood Cliffs, NJ, 1984, pp. 151–160; Kevin W. Kelley (Ed.), *The Home Planet*, Addison Wesley Pub., Reading, MA, 1988; Jeannye Thornton, "Moon Rooms?" *U.S. News & World Report* (June 1, 1998), p. 12. Copyright 1998, *U.S. News & World Report.* **Unit 6, Lecture 12:** Suzanne Hamlin, "Science May Help Green Tea Get Steeped in U.S. Culture," *The OC Register* (June 30, 1994), p. 9; "Reading Tea Leaves for Health Benefits," *Tufts University Diet and Nutrition Letter,* 13:8 (October 1995), p. 4. Reprinted with permission: Tufts Health & Nutrition letter; "Can Green Tea Help Prevent Cancer?" *University of California at Berkeley Wellness Letter*, 14:3 (Dec. 1997), pp. 1–2. **Unit 6, Lecture 13:** K. C. Cole, "Vetoing the Way America Votes," *Los Angeles Times* (August 16, 1995), pp. A1, A10. Copyright © 1995 *Los Angeles Times.* Reprinted by permission; James MacGregor Burns, J. W. Peltason, and Thomas E. Cronin, *Government by the People, 12th alt. ed.*, Prentice Hall Inc., Englewood Cliffs, NJ, 1985, pp. 195–199. **Unit 6, Lecture 14:** Philip Yenawine, *How to Look at Modern Art,* Harry N. Abrams Inc. Pub., New York, 1991, pp. 143–144. **Unit 6, Lecture 15:** Jane E. Stevens, "Cybersurgery," *Los Angeles Times* (December 4, 1995), p. B2. Copyright © 1995 *Los Angeles Times.* Reprinted by permission; David R. Olmos, "Is There a Robot in the House?" *Los Angeles Times* (July 14, 1997), p. D1; Kathy A. Svitil, "Robotic Surgery," *Discover* (July 1998), p. 28. Copyright © 1998. Reprinted with permission of *Discover Magazine*; **Unit 6, Lecture 16:** Frederick K. Lutgens and Edward J. Tarbuck, *Foundations of Earth Science,* Prentice Hall, Upper Saddle River, NJ, 1996; Frederick K. Lutgens and Edward J. Tarbuck, *Essentials of Geology, 6e*, Prentice Hall, Upper Saddle River, NJ, 1998, p. 292. Reprinted by permission of Prentice Hall; Richard C. Paddock and Robert Lee Hotz, "Warning from Space?" *Los Angeles Times* (April 9, 1998), p. B2. Copyright © 1998 *Los Angeles Times.* Reprinted by permission; Terry R. West, *Geology Applied to Engineering*, Prentice Hall, NJ, 1994. **Unit 6, Lecture 17:** Elizabeth Hall, "How Cultures Collide," *Psychology Today* (July 1976), pp. 66–74; Kurien Joseph, "Cultural Differences in International Business," *Export Import Trade Flash* (Oct. 1–15, 1997).

⊞ Photos

⊞ Illustrations

$$\boxed{1}$$

PRE-COURSEWORK EVALUATION

◑ Goals

- Evaluate listening comprehension skills
- Evaluate note-taking skills
- Evaluate ability to note numbers

◑ Questions for Discussion

- What problems do you have when you listen to a lecture in English?
- Do you have any of these problems when you listen to a lecture in your native language?
- In your opinion, what are the sources of these problems?

▤ Evaluating Listening Comprehension and Note-Taking Skills

In this unit, you will listen to two parts of a short lecture about lecture comprehension and a dictation of numbers. You will practice taking notes and using your notes to complete a chart or answer comprehension questions. After each activity, you will evaluate your listening comprehension and note-taking ability. To get a sense of your listening and note-taking skills, your teacher will also evaluate your notes and your answers.

1 THE PROCESS OF LECTURE COMPREHENSION

PART 1

The first part of the lecture focuses on the differences between listening to lectures and listening in everyday situations. Take notes on a separate piece of paper as if you were in a class and were responsible for the material covered in the lecture. When you have finished, use your notes to complete the chart below.

	Lecture	Everyday Listening Situation
Language		
Interaction		
Expectations		

Self-Evaluation

When you have completed the chart, answer the following questions.

1. How would you describe your ability to comprehend the lecture?
   _____ Excellent _____ Very Good _____ Good _____ Fair _____ Poor
2. How would you describe your ability to take notes while listening to the lecture?
   _____ Excellent _____ Very Good _____ Good _____ Fair _____ Poor

PART 2

The second part of the lecture focuses on tasks that students need to do while listening to lectures. Take notes on a separate piece of paper as if you were in a class and were responsible for the material covered in the lecture. When you have finished, use your notes to answer the following comprehension questions.

1. What are the four things that a listener needs to do in order to comprehend a lecture efficiently?

   a. _____

   b. _____

   c. _____

   d. _____

2. In addition to words, what other features of language carry meaning?

   a. _____   c. _____

   b. _____   d. _____

3. Give two reasons why listeners must predict while listening to lectures.

   a. _____

   b. _____

4. There are two types of predictions that people make when listening to a lecture. What are they?

   a. _____   b. _____

5. To add information to the lecturer's words, what kind of knowledge do listeners use?

   a. _____   b. _____

6. Give two reasons why listeners must evaluate while listening to lectures.

   a. _____

   b. _____

Self-Evaluation

When you have finished answering the comprehension questions, answer the following questions.

1. How would you describe your ability to comprehend the lecture?
   _____ Excellent   _____ Very Good   _____ Good   _____ Fair   _____ Poor

2. How would you describe your ability to take notes while listening to the lecture?
   _____ Excellent   _____ Very Good   _____ Good   _____ Fair   _____ Poor

POST-LECTURE DISCUSSION

Discuss the following questions in small groups.

1. According to the information that you heard in Parts 1 and 2 of the lecture, why might nonnative speakers of English have a hard time listening to lectures and taking notes?

2. In your opinion, what do you need to change or improve in order to be a better listener and note-taker?

DICTATION OF NUMBERS

You will hear statements containing numbers. Write the numbers that you hear.

1. Michelangelo: born in _____

2. Georgia O'Keeffe: born in _____ ; died in _____

3. 1 cup raisins: _____ calories

4. One slice of white bread: _____ calories

5. Zipper: invented in _____

6. Piano: invented in _____

7. Microscope: invented in _____

8. Missouri River: _____ miles long

9. Diameter of Earth: _____ miles

10. Mount Everest: _____ feet high

11. Sahara Desert:_____ square miles

12. Earth's distance from sun: _____ miles

13. Pluto's distance from sun: _____ miles

14. Tokyo's projected population in 2015: _____

15. One pound: _____ grams

16. An earthquake occurred in Iran on _____ .

17. This earthquake measured _____ on the Richter scale and caused _____ deaths and _____ injuries.

18. Length of board: _____ feet; width: _____ inches; depth: _____ inch

Self-Evaluation

When you have finished the dictation, answer the following questions.

1. How would you describe your ability to comprehend the numbers?
____ Excellent ____ Very Good ____ Good ____ Fair ____ Poor

2. How would you describe your ability to note the numbers?
____ Excellent ____ Very Good ____ Good ____ Fair ____ Poor

Your teacher will use a form similar to the one below when commenting on your notes in this class.

Note-Taking Feedback Form

Name _____

Date _____ Lecture _____

ORGANIZATION OF IDEAS*

____ You organize while you write. Good.

____ Your notes visually represent the relationship between ideas. Good.

____ Your notes reflect some attempt at visually representing the relationship between ideas. Keep working on that.

____ Your notes are unclear in that it is not possible to quickly see the relationship between ideas. Work on organizing your notes so that the important ideas stand out and the relationships between ideas are clear. Use the space on the page to show how pieces of information relate to other pieces of information (through indenting or connecting lines, for example). Use headings to show how ideas relate to one another.

____ Your notes reflect random noting of words. Evaluate as you listen to get the main points that the speaker is trying to communicate. Focus on these main points and add details when you have time or when rewriting notes.

____ You seem to be trying to note down every word. Focus on noting the minimum number of "key words" that would carry the same meaning. This will allow you more time during listening and note-taking for comprehending and evaluating ideas.

Additional comments about organization: _____

_____

_____

ACCURACY AND COMPLETENESS OF NOTES*

____ You seem to get most points, both major and minor ones. Good.

____ You seem to get most points (especially the major ones) but miss or misinterpret (a few/many) minor ones. It's good that you are able to discriminate between major ideas and minor ones. Practice and increased fluency in English will help you note more details.

____ You miss or misinterpret (a few/many) major ideas and (a few/many) minor ideas. Keep the "larger picture" in mind as you listen. Focus on getting the major points that the lecturer is trying to communicate first. When you have time, note details related to these major points.

---

* Chapters 3 and 5 in this book introduce these skills.

_____ You may be noting too few "key words" to allow you to retain the full meaning from the lecture. These notes would probably not be helpful later. Revise or rewrite your notes as soon as possible after lectures so that you can expand your notes with information that you remember.

Additional comments about accuracy and completeness of notes:

_____

_____

_____

ACCURACY OF NOTING NUMBERS*

_____ You seem to be able to note most numbers. Good.
_____ You miss or misinterpret a few numbers.
_____ You miss or misinterpret many numbers.

Additional comments about accuracy of noting numbers:

_____

_____

_____

OVERALL EVALUATION:

_____

_____

_____

_____

_____

_____

_____

_____

_____

_____

_____

_____

---

* Chapter 4 introduces this skill.

2

LOOKING AT LECTURE TRANSCRIPTS

◗ Goals

- Increase awareness of how lectures are formulated
- Increase ability to predict information, including content and organizational direction

Comparing the Language of Lecturing to the Language of Writing

In this section, you will look at excerpts from authentic lectures. These excerpts are written the way the lecturers gave them. Therefore, you may find some incomplete sentences, tangents, and "uhs" and "ahs." You will see that the language in lectures is very different from the language in magazines or books. You can see some examples of this in the following excerpt from a lecture about a sociolinguistic perspective on language.

Let's first look at one aspect of language . . . I want to look at the sociological or sociolinguistic way of looking at language . . . all right . . . from this point of view some linguists have come up with the idea that language is a game . . . like football, soccer, baseball . . . each person who speaks in any particular language or any community knows all the rules of this game . . . they know how to play . . . somebody who comes from a different one . . . as you know well . . . may not know all the rules . . . so you have some problems with communication . . . now because we said language is a game doesn't necessarily mean that we play it for fun . . . we usually play it for serious reasons . . . most of the time . . . although sometimes we tell jokes and things like that . . . hmmm . . . I seem to do that quite often in this class . . . but the rules . . . no matter what we do . . . are very well defined . . . you may not know what they are . . . but they're very clear rules of what you can do and what you can't do in any situation . . .

If this excerpt were to be written for a magazine, it would look very different. It might look like this:

One way to look at language is through a sociological or sociolinguistic perspective. In this view, language is seen as a game in which each person in a particular language community knows all the rules. Unlike recreational games, however, this game is taken very seriously.

Exercise

Compare the lecture excerpt to the magazine paragraph. Write down the ways that they differ.

Lecture Excerpt	Magazine Paragraph

Recognizing Cues

CUES TO TOPIC INTRODUCTIONS

When you compared the language used in a magazine to the language used in a lecture, you may have noticed that, in the lecture excerpt, you are given explicit (stated) directions about what to look at or listen for.

Example

cues to topic introduction

(Let's first look at) one aspect of language . . . (I want to look at) the sociolog-

ical or sociolinguistic way of looking at language . . .

We can call these directions "cues." They direct you to listen to something. The words noted in the example are cues to topic introductions. Some cues to topic introductions are specific, such as "Let's look at X," "Today we're going to talk about X," or "OK. Let's move on to X." Other topic introduction cues may not be as specific, but they still give you a hint that the speaker is starting a new idea.

The expressions "all right" and "now" sometimes indicate a topic introduction.

Examples

(All right) . . . from this point of view some linguists have come up with the

idea that language is a game . . .

possible cues to topic introduction

(Now) because we said language is a game doesn't necessarily mean that we

play it for fun . . .

Note that "all right" and "now" do not *always* indicate a topic introduction. They sometimes have other meanings and functions.

Another cue to topic introduction is the rhetorical question.

Example

cue to topic introduction

(You might ask . . . well . . . how did the researchers judge psychological

distress?) . . . they used five measures . . . the first measure was . . .

The lecturer, when posing a rhetorical question, does not expect a response from the audience. Rather, the lecturer is introducing a new topic.

Another cue to topic introduction is a one- or two-word summary of the upcoming information spoken with statement intonation.

Example

OK. Definitions.

In written text, these cues to topic introduction are not needed. For one thing, written text is permanent. The reader can reread the words to better understand what the writer is trying to say. Secondly, written text is organized so that paragraphs generally focus on one main idea. The reader can find main ideas by looking for topic sentences or thesis statements. The indentation of a new paragraph generally tells the reader that a new idea is beginning.

CUES TO ORGANIZATION

When writers write, they consider how they can organize their ideas in order to present them most clearly. Writers use words such as "the first example," "the second example," "on the other hand," and so on. Lecturers also use these cues to organization when they speak so that their listeners can more easily understand their ideas and how they relate to each other.

Example

cues to organization
Let's first look at (one aspect) of language . . . basically some linguists have set up (five categories). . .

What do you expect the lecturer to do later on in this lecture?

These cues to organization help you make predictions about how the lecture will be organized. Notice how many cues to organization are in the next lecture excerpt (from the same lecture on language).

Basically some linguists have set up (five categories) of accomplishing things . . . we use language to describe . . . tell about the world that we see . . . there's a chair over there . . . there's a person over here . . . someone is from China . . . or whatever . . . (another thing) that we use it for is to tell people to do something . . . please close the door . . . please open the door . . . do your homework . . . do this . . . do that . . . now we might not always say do it but we have ways of telling people to do something . . . (another way) . . . (a third way) . . . is we use language to tell people what we're going to do . . . I'm going to tell you about language . . . I'm going to open the door . . . (another way) to look at language . . . (two other ways) . . . one is to tell about feelings . . . express what's inside of us about the world . . . not only that there is a chair but that I don't like that chair or I do like that chair . . . (and the fifth way) or (the fifth thing) we use is to change the world . . . certain things that you say change the world . . . if I say you fail this course . . . that language changes the world . . . just my four words make you unhappy and hate me . . . something has changed because of my words and nothing else except those words . . . so we can change the world with language . . . now since we have all these different purposes and you probably can think of other purposes with which we want to use language to win or accomplish what we want inside . . . so it's kind of like a game that way.

CUES TO TOPIC CONCLUSIONS

Look back at the lecture excerpt that you just read. Notice that when the lecturer has finished describing the five categories, he then attempts to tie the preceding ideas together by saying, " . . . now since we have all these different purposes and you probably can think of other purposes with which we want to use language to win or accomplish what we want inside . . . so it's kind of like a game that way."

What kind of cues were used to indicate this topic completion? For one thing, the speaker used reference words to group all the preceding information together by saying, "We have *all these different purposes.*" This indicated a break from his previous goal of describing each of the five categories. In addition, the speaker preceded the summary with a pause and the cue "now." ("Now" may indicate the beginning of a summary as well as a new idea.) Finally, the lecturer emphasized the conclusion of that topic in the last line, "*so* we have all these different purposes." Words such as "so," "therefore," and "thus" often signal a topic conclusion.

⊞ Recognizing Paraphrase, Repetition, Exemplification, and Tangential Information

Have you ever heard anyone read aloud a journal article or thesis (or any piece of writing that was originally meant to be read silently)? It is often very difficult to follow. That is because in written language there is much less repetition and paraphrase than in spoken language.

Compare the amount of paraphrase, repetition, and exemplification in the first lecture excerpt to that in the magazine paragraph on page 8. This is a very important difference between the language of lectures and the language of writing. When writing, writers only need to state an idea once because they know that the readers can reread an idea as many times as they want. However, when listening, often words can "go in one ear and out the other." Therefore, the lecturer needs to give the listeners time to process or take notes on what they have heard. Lecturers do this by repeating their ideas in different ways (i.e., paraphrasing), repeating their ideas in exactly the same words, or expanding upon their ideas in greater detail (e.g., by giving examples). Paraphrase, repetition, and exemplification do not add new ideas; they simply give the listener time to better understand the speaker's ideas.

Lecturers also go off on tangents, or go off the topic, more often than writers do. This is because lectures are live events, and lecturers may express unplanned thoughts while speaking. In addition, lecturers often try to connect with their audience in a more personal way, and this may result in a tangent. Writers have the option of editing their tangents; lecturers do not.

Re-examine the excerpt from the lecture about a sociolinguistic perspective on language. Notice how much of the excerpt is repetition, paraphrase, support for a main idea, or tangential to the main idea.

Let's first look at one aspect of language . . . I want to look at the sociological

or sociolinguistic way of looking at language . . . all right . . . from this

point of view some linguists have come up with the idea that language is a
examples
game . . . *like football, soccer, baseball* . . . each person who speaks in any

particular language or any community knows all the rules of this game . . .
—paraphrase
they know how to play . . . somebody who comes from a different one . . .

as you know well . . . may not know all the rules . . . so you have some

problems with communication . . . now because we said language is a

game doesn't necessarily mean that we play it for fun . . . we usually play
tangent
it for serious reasons . . . most of the time . . . *although sometimes we tell*

jokes and things like that . . . hmmm . . . I seem to do that quite often in

this class . . . but the rules . . . no matter what we do . . . are very well
paraphrase
defined . . . *you may not know what they are* . . . *but they're very clear*

rules of what you can do and what you can't do in any situation . . .

☐ Summarizing Key Differences between the Language of Lecturing and the Language of Writing

There are many differences between the language used for lecturing and the language used for writing. For example, different vocabulary is used. Also, written language uses punctuation to separate and relate ideas, while spoken language uses a type of vocal punctuation (e.g., hesitations and intonation) to achieve the same purpose. Two major differences that are especially important for note-taking concern the use of cues and the use of paraphrase, repetition, exemplification, and tangential information.

- Lecturers use verbal and nonverbal cues to indicate the introduction of new ideas, a change of topic, the conclusion of an idea, and the intended organization. Listeners depend on these cues to follow the lecture.
- Lecturers use more paraphrasing, repetition, and exemplification than writers. They may expand on ideas more in order to allow the listeners more time to process important information. They are also more likely to go off on tangents if new thoughts arise while they are speaking.

Exercise

The purpose of this exercise is to identify cues and extra information in a lecture excerpt. This can help you understand the overall organization and recognize the main ideas. The following excerpt includes both parts of the lecture about a socio-linguistic perspective on language that we have already examined.

Directions

1. Read the entire excerpt. Try to get a sense of what the lecturer is saying.
2. Circle all the cues.
3. Cross out all repetitions, paraphrases, examples, and tangents.
4. When you have finished, compare your choices with those of a classmate. Discuss why you marked what you did. Your answers don't have to be exactly the same, but you should be able to explain why you marked the excerpt the way that you did. The first half of the exercise has been done for you.

cue to topic introduction   *cue to organization*   *cue to topic introduction*

(Let's first look at) (one aspect) of language . . . (I want to look at) the sociolog-

ical or sociolinguistic way of looking at language . . . all right . . . from this

point of view some linguists have come up with the idea that language is a

game . . . ~~like football, soccer, baseball~~ . . . each person who speaks in any

particular language or any community knows all the rules of this game . . .

~~they know how to play~~ . . . somebody who comes from a different one . . .

as you know well . . . may not know all the rules . . . so you have some

problems with communication . . . now because we said language is a

game doesn't necessarily mean that we play it for fun . . . we usually play

it for serious reasons . . . most of the time . . . although sometimes we do play it for fun . . . ~~sometimes we tell jokes and things like that . . . hmmm . . . I seem to do that quite often in this class~~ . . . but the rules . . . no matter what we do . . . are very well defined . . . ~~you may not know what they are . . . but they're very clear rules of what you can do and what you can't do in any situation~~ . . . usually in any use of language people are trying to accomplish something . . . ~~trying to do something~~ . . . that's why they talk . . . ~~sometimes you just talk to yourself for no reason . . . some crazy people talk for no reason but most people talk because they want to accomplish something~~ . . . basically some linguists have set up (five categories) of

cue to organization

accomplishing things . . . we use language to describe . . . tell about the world that we see . . . there's a chair over there . . . there's a person over here . . . someone is from China . . . or whatever . . . another thing that we use it for is to tell people to do something . . . please close the door . . . please open the door . . . do your homework . . . do this . . . do that . . . now we might not always say do it but we have ways of telling people to do something . . . another way . . . a third way . . . is we use language to tell people what we're going to do . . . I'm going to tell you about language . . . I'm going to open the door . . . another way to look at language . . . two other ways . . . one is to tell about feelings . . . express what's inside of us about the world . . . not only that there is a chair but that I don't like that chair or I do like that chair . . . and the fifth way or the fifth thing we use is to change the world . . . certain things that you say change the world . . . if I say you fail this course . . . that language changes the world . . . just my four words make you unhappy and hate me . . . something has changed because of my words and nothing else except those words . . . so we can change the world with language . . . now since we have all these different purposes and you probably can think of other purposes with which we want to use language to win or accomplish what we want inside . . . so it's kind of like a game that way.

▣ Getting the Main Ideas Using Context and Prediction

Listeners use the cues in lectures to predict how the lecture is going to continue. They also use the context to predict missing words and ideas.

To understand the main ideas, you do not need to catch every word. While listening to a lecture, it is easy to miss words because your mind wanders, you

are busy taking notes, you misunderstand something, or you don't know the vocabulary. In addition, the lecturer might be speaking too quickly or not saying every word clearly. The microphone might even be functioning poorly. However, this does not mean that you cannot understand the main ideas of the lecture. You can use logic, your knowledge of the subject, and your understanding of lecture cues to make good guesses about information that you might have missed.

Exercise

The purpose of this exercise is to demonstrate that you can get the main ideas of a lecture even if you don't understand every word and idea. The following excerpt is a later part of the lecture about a sociolinguistic perspective on language. Many words and ideas have been omitted. In some cases, you may be able to guess what has been left out; in other cases, you may not be sure.

Directions

1. Read the entire excerpt. Try to get an idea of what it is about. Do not spend time trying to figure out the missing word(s); just try to make sense of what you are reading.
2. Answer the question that follows the lecture.
3. Compare your answers with those of a classmate. If your answers differ, explain your reasons to each other.

> Now language is also like a game in a number of other ways . . . basically
>
> like a game . . . you usually need more than _____ person to play lan-
>
> guage . . . usually _____ talk to somebody else or _____ group of
>
> people . . . sometimes you talk to yourself but that's more _____ than
>
> usual except if you're thinking not outright talking . . . it's a game because

it's ▓▓▓▓▓ . . . something that we ▓▓▓▓▓ together . . . another way it's
like a ▓▓▓▓▓ is that the players ▓▓▓▓▓ . . . one person ▓▓▓▓▓ and a
new person comes into the ▓▓▓▓▓ . . . three or four people are standing
together . . . they may all be playing . . . one may leave and a substitute
▓▓▓▓▓ . . . so it's like a game in that way . . . another thing is of course
like I said, you're out to win something just like ▓▓▓▓▓▓▓▓▓▓▓
▓▓▓▓▓▓▓▓▓▓▓▓▓▓ . . . we're usually out to accom-
plish something . . . something tangible . . . or something intangible . . .
like emotional satisfaction . . . something to that effect . . . OK . . . another
thing is that everybody has his own style of ▓▓▓▓▓ like
▓▓▓▓▓▓▓▓▓▓▓▓▓▓ . . . just like that some
speakers are very good at certain ways of speaking and have certain individual styles of speaking . . . everybody is ▓▓▓▓▓ . . . nobody speaks
the same . . . also, like a soccer player or like any game player you can
change your style . . . ▓▓▓▓▓▓▓▓▓▓▓▓▓▓
▓▓▓▓▓ . . . so styles change as well as the fact that each person has his
own style . . . all right and the last thing is that we have rules for the
game . . . just like we have rules now in the classroom . . . when I talk,
you ▓▓▓▓▓ unless I give you some signal that says it's time for you to
talk or I stop talking . . . there are very definite rules for not interrupting
and ▓▓▓▓▓▓▓ . . . and for all kinds of things . . . we all know
these rules but we probably ▓▓▓▓▓▓▓▓▓▓▓▓▓▓ . . .
when you're talking about football you can say it's played in a field so big
so wide . . . you can't kick the ball off the field . . . it has many rules and
everybody can learn those ▓▓▓▓▓ and tell us what they are . . . language
is a little different . . . if I asked you for some of the rules of language . . .
you may not be able to state them explicitly . . . but there are very definite
rules and we all know what they are . . . the only time problems come in is
when you know Chinese or Korean rules and I know American rules and
we don't ▓▓▓▓▓▓▓ . . . then we have ▓▓▓▓▓▓ and lack
of communication . . . we don't ▓▓▓▓▓▓▓▓▓ . . . for
example . . . if you know football and you try to play with the rules of a
soccer game . . . of course ▓▓▓▓▓▓▓▓▓▓▓▓ . . .
you're not going to be able to accomplish what you want to accomplish . . .
so in terms of the sociolinguistic way of looking at language . . . language

is a kind of rule-governed behavior . . . of interaction between people . . . like a ▓▓▓▓ . . . everybody knows the ▓▓▓▓ . . . they're mutually intelligible . . . we all know within a given community . . . ▓▓▓▓▓▓▓ knows how to play . . . . even if we cannot explicitly state the rules . . . now the big question for you probably and for me if we're trying to learn a language . . . how can I learn the rules of the other language? . . . so part of the definition . . . we can say . . . a rule-governed social behavior . . . is one way of looking at language from a sociological kind of viewpoint.

The lecturer suggests a number of ways that language is like a game. What are they?

Example

You usually need more than one person to "play." _____

1. _____

2. _____

3. _____

4. _____

5. _____

Predicting Content and Lecture Direction

Predicting content and lecture direction helps you to organize your notes in advance and to listen more selectively and efficiently. Predicting does not mean knowing the correct answer; it means making an educated guess.

Exercise

The purpose of this exercise is to demonstrate that you can predict content and lecture direction. The following excerpt is from a lecture about women and work. At twelve different points, you will be directed to stop reading and predict what will come next. (**Tip:** Cover each section of the lecture until you are ready to read it. Don't read ahead until you have stopped and made a prediction.)

All over the world the question of women's role in society is becoming . . . or *is* an emotionally charged issue . . . women are questioning their previous roles *and* exploring new roles . . . everyone seems to have an opinion about it . . . one good thing that has come out of this is that women now feel that they have control or more control over the direction of their lives . . . but this has caused some conflict . . . in fact . . . some people are saying that there is more strain on women than ever before . . . in any case . . . at least in the United States and many other countries . . . women must now decide a major question . . .

Stop and Predict

Whether to work outside of the home . . . pursue a career . . . or whether to stay at home and raise a family or whether to do both . . . I must add that this is the dilemma of a lucky few women . . . here in the United States nowadays the majority of working women must work outside and it is no longer a luxury . . . but anyway what I would like to focus on in this lecture are some of the factors a woman might want to take into account when deciding whether to enter the job market or not . . .

Stop and Predict

A major question would be which one is emotionally and physically more beneficial . . .

Stop and Predict

Let me first look at the physical side of the question . . .

Stop and Predict

Previously we knew that men had a higher heart-attack rate than women did . . . and that most people blamed that on the fact that they worked outside of the home and women didn't . . . work in the job market being more stressful than staying at home . . . however . . .

Stop and Predict

Now with more than 50 percent of women in the job market and still there is an uneven heart-attack rate. . . . this theory has lost credibility . . . in fact research has shown that women who work outside the home appear to be at no greater risk than women who stay at home . . . for heart disease at least . . . so . . .

Stop and Predict

It seems that physically there is no benefit . . . in working outside the home or not . . . they seem to be about equal . . . but . . . what about the emotional side of the question?

Stop and Predict

I'd like to tell you about a study that was done at three universities and colleges which compared women working in the job market to housewives . . . the employed women . . . whose mean age was thirty-three . . . ranged from secretaries to professionals and executives . . . most of the women in both groups were college educated . . . now the test was designed to study who was emotionally stronger . . . the women in the job market or the housewives . . . the researchers defined emotional strength as . . . the degree . . . of psychological distress . . . to which someone . . . reacts . . . to a life crisis . . . let me repeat that . . . the degree . . . of psychological distress . . . to which someone . . . reacts . . . to a life crisis . . . in other words how much psychological distress did they show when there was a crisis in their lives? . . . you might ask well how did the researchers judge psychological distress? . . .

Stop and Predict

They used five measures . . . the first measure was anxiety . . . how much anxiety did the woman report in her life? . . . how often did she complain of anxiety? . . . the second one . . . irritability . . . how often did she complain of being irritated? . . . the third one . . . somatic complaints . . .

somatic meaning bodily . . . complaints relating to the body . . . in other words . . . how often did the woman complain about having headaches or backaches? . . . the fourth one . . . depression . . . how often did the woman complain about being depressed? feeling depressed? . . . the fifth one was problems in thinking and concentrating . . . how often did the woman complain about having this sort of problem? . . . added together these measures formed a way of judging how much psychological distress was in someone's life . . . what did the researchers find? . . .

Stop and Predict

First of all they found that housewives generally experience lower levels of stressful life events than employed women do . . . yet . . .

Stop and Predict

They seem to react to life crises with more psychological distress than employed women do . . . that is . . .

Stop and Predict

They have less stress in their lives yet they show more psychological distress . . . to put it from the employed women's perspective . . . the employed women have more stress in their lives both at work and in their marriages yet they show fewer signs of psychological distress . . . this test seems to imply quite a lot . . .

Stop and Predict

It implies that employment may equip women better for coping with stressful life events than does staying at home . . . the researchers caution that other factors such as social class . . . job status . . . may contribute to these differences . . . and that the results may apply only to certain types of women in certain situations.

How did you do? Were you able to predict the direction of the lecture at least some of the time? If so, that's good. Once again, predicting does not mean getting the right answer; it means making an educated guess.

3

NOTE-TAKING BASICS

⟩ Goals

- Learn how to choose key words to note
- Learn how to judge the relative importance of information
- Learn how to visually represent the relationship between pieces of information

Noting Key Words

When you take notes, you do not have time to write down everything that the speaker says. You must note as much information as possible in the fewest words. Omit the words that are not important. Write down only key words, or words that carry meaning. Develop your own symbols and abbreviations. The important thing is that you understand your notes and are able to read them a day, a week, or a year later.

Notice how key words are noted in the following example.

Lecturer: John F. Kennedy was the thirty-fifth president of the
              United States.
Notes: JFK — 35th pres. of U.S.

JFK are initials that are familiar to most Americans, so it makes sense to use them. Compare the following two sets of notes.

Lecturer: Dan Quayle was George Bush's vice-president.
Good Notes: Quayle — Bush's V.P.
Poor Notes: DQ — GB's V.P.

What is wrong with the second example? The initials DQ and GB are not familiar, and I would not know what they meant if I read my notes later. I am, however, familiar with V.P., the abbreviation for vice-president.

Using Note-Taking Symbols and Abbreviations

Symbols can replace words that show relationships. For example, the dash (—) can symbolize the verb "was" or any other form of "to be."

Example
JFK — 35th pres. of U.S. = John F. Kennedy *was* the 35th president of
                          the United States.

Here are some other symbols that you might use:

=	equals	/	per
≠	does not equal	~	approximately; circa
&	and	$\overrightarrow{1929}$	since 1929
>	is more than	$\overleftarrow{1929}$	1929 and earlier
<	is less than	c.	century
$	money	w/	with
↗	to go up; to increase	w/o	without
↓	to go down; to decrease	♂	man; men
→	leading to; heading toward	♀	woman; women
∴	therefore; so	e.g.	for example
∵	because	" "	(repeated words)
"	inches	#	number
'	feet; minutes	i.e.	that is; in other words
°	degree	%	percent
@	at	+	plus

Do you use any other symbols? Share them with the class. Note any additional symbols that you would like to remember in the space below.

Exercise

You will hear ten short statements. Take notes in as few words as possible. Use note-taking symbols and abbreviations where appropriate. When you have finished, compare your notes in small groups.

Example
Lecturer: The demand for oil has increased greatly in the past 100 years, so the price has also risen.
Notes: demand for oil ↑ in past 100 yrs. ∴ price ↑

Visually Representing Relationships and the Relative Importance of Information

Another way to increase the amount of information in your notes is to use the space on your paper to show relationships and the relative importance of information.

Example

Lecturer: The three largest states in the United States are Texas, Alaska, and California. Texas is located in the south-central part of the United States and is on the border of Mexico. Alaska is located to the northwest of Canada, and California is on the western coast of the continental United States.

Notes: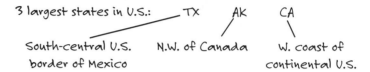

or

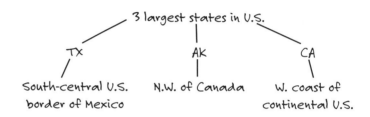

Notice how the arrangement of the notes clearly shows which information relates to the particular topic. It also clearly shows how the lecture is organized; that is, it shows the three largest states in the United States and then gives information about each one.

Indentation is another way to show the relationships between pieces of information and their relative importance. Write the most general information farthest to the left. Write more specific information under the general information and indent it toward the right.

Example

Lecturer: A poll was taken recently surveying twelve hundred adults in the United States to find out what they considered important in their lives. Ninety-six percent said that having a good family life was important. Ninety-five percent said that using their mind and abilities was important. This latter quality was most important to women beginning work careers. This priority marks a shift in the type of work people are involved in—moving away from physical labor and toward jobs requiring mental skills.

Notes: poll—1,200 Americans—What is important in your life?
    96%—have good family life
    95%—use mind and abilities
        most important to ♀ beginning careers
        shows shift in work habits → jobs requiring mental
            skills, not physical labor

There are other ways to arrange this information into notes. In all cases, make sure that you use as few words as possible and accurately express the lecturer's ideas in terms of importance of information and relationship between pieces of information.

Exercise

You will hear twelve short statements. Take informative notes in as few words as possible. Use symbols, abbreviations, key words, indentation, and connecting lines where appropriate. When you have finished, compare your notes in small groups.

2 WOMEN AND WORK

 In Unit 2, you practiced predicting content and lecture direction while reading a transcript of a lecture on women and work. You will now listen to the entire lecture. While listening, look at the example notes below.

Major ? — ♀ work outside? stay home? both?

Which is emotionally   and   physically more beneficial?

study — 3 univ. & colleges compare   in past, ♂ had higher

employed ♀ & housewives   heart-attack rate

     mean age 33   perhaps because

     sec'y & prof.   worked outside?

     most college ed.

     designed to see who was emotionally stronger   BUT — now 50+% ♀ in jobs

         & still uneven rate

Emotional strength: degree of psych distress to

which someone reacts to a life crisis.   NO BENEFIT in work

         outside or not (about =)

How judge?

     1. anxiety

     2. irritability

     3. somatic (body) complaints

     4. depression

     5. problems in thinking and concentrating

Results?

     Housewives — ↓ levels of stress in lives YET react to crises w/ ↑ distress

     Employed ♀ — ↑ stress in lives YET show ↓ distress

Implies?

     employment equips ♀ for coping w/ stress better

(Results may apply to only some ♀ , not all)

Did you notice the following?

- The notes visually represent the organization of the lecture and the relative importance of pieces of information in the lecture.
- The major points are written farthest to the left, with details indented under the generalizations that they support.
- The major issue—whether work outside the home is emotionally or physically beneficial or harmful to women—stands out. There is information about the emotional side of the problem in one area of the page and information about the physical side of the problem in another.
- Headings such as "Results?" and "Implies?" help to organize the notes by clarifying the purpose of important sections.

NOTE-TAKING PRACTICE

Listen to the lecture again. Without looking at the example, take notes. Use symbols, abbreviations, key words, indentation, connecting lines, and headings where appropriate.

Eight DOs and DON'Ts for Improving Lecture Comprehension and Note-Taking

1. DON'T note every word.	DO note key words.
2. DON'T write everything down.	DO use abbreviations and symbols.
3. DON'T note indiscriminately.	DO evaluate as you listen. Decide what is important and what is not.
4. DON'T take notes as if you were writing a composition.	DO use the space on your paper to organize information and visually represent the relationship between ideas.
5. DON'T be a passive listener.	DO be an active listener. Predict lecture content and organization.
6. DON'T give up if you miss information.	DO make guesses if you miss information. Remember that lecturers usually repeat and paraphrase information.
7. DON'T lose sight of the forest for the trees. (Don't listen for details before getting the larger picture.)	DO listen for the lecturer's main points and for the general organizational framework.
8. DON'T forget about your notes when you leave the lecture.	DO rewrite and/or revise your notes as soon as possible after the lecture. That way, ideas that you did not have time to note will still be fresh in your mind, and you will be able to add them. In addition, you can reorganize information so that the ideas are more clearly and accurately represented.

4

NOTING NUMBERS AND STATISTICS

▷ Goals

- Learn how to recognize the differences between numbers that sound similar
- Learn how to comprehend and note large numbers, fractions, decimals, and dates
- Practice noting numbers, dates, and statistics while listening to lectures

Differentiating between Numbers That Sound Similar

Hearing the difference between numbers such as 14 and 40 requires paying attention to differences in stress. Listen to the following numbers.

14 fourteen	40 forty	17 seventeen	70 seventy
15 fifteen	50 fifty	18 eighteen	80 eighty
16 sixteen	60 sixty	19 nineteen	90 ninety

Exercise A

 You will hear ten numbers. Circle the numbers that you hear.

Example

13   (30)   33

1.	13	30	33		6.	18	80	8
2.	14	40	4		7.	19	90	9
3.	15	50	5		8.	14	40	4
4.	16	60	6		9.	16	60	6
5.	17	70	7		10.	18	80	8

Exercise B

 You will hear five numbers. Write the numbers that you hear.

1. _____   4. _____

2. _____   5. _____

3. _____

▦ Noting Years

Notice the following ways to present years.

1300 B.C.	thirteen hundred B.C.
A.D. 1492	A.D. fourteen (hundred and) ninety-two
1902	nineteen oh two
2000	two thousand
2002	two thousand (and) two
14th c.	1300–1399; the fourteenth century
the 60s	(the decade of) the sixties, the nineteen sixties, 1960–1969

Exercise

You will hear ten years. Write the years that you hear.

1. _____   6. _____

2. _____   7. _____

3. _____   8. _____

4. _____   9. _____

5. _____   10. _____

⊞ Noting Large Numbers in Isolation

Noting large numbers requires familiarity with the English number system. Look at the number 12,506,825,001.

12,	506,	825,	001
Billions	Millions	Thousands	Ones

Remember that numbers are in groups of three digits, except for the group farthest to the left. A hint is to write a comma (,) every time you hear a word such as "billion," "million," or "thousand."

The group-of-three concept is very important for numbers such as 100,001. The zeros are necessary to hold the places in the group. In this case, the number 100 is in the thousands group and the number 1 is in the ones group. The ones group has three places; therefore, the number 1 must be written as 001.

Exercise A

 You will hear ten numbers. Circle the numbers that you hear.

1.	102	120	1,002
2.	115	150	1,050
3.	1,020	1,200	1,002
4.	1,252	1,250	1,025
5.	3,560	3,516	3,056
6.	53,000	50,300	503,000
7.	407,000	470,000	47,000
8.	1,213,000	1,000,213,000	1,213,000,000
9.	5,000,020	5,000,200	5,020,000
10.	16,010,001	16,000,001	16,100,010

Exercise B

 You will hear ten numbers. Write the numbers that you hear.

1. _____   6. _____
2. _____   7. _____
3. _____   8. _____
4. _____   9. _____
5. _____   10. _____

Noting Fractions and Decimals

Notice the following ways to say fractions and decimals.

½	one-half
⅔	two-thirds
¾	three-quarters *or* three-fourths
⅞	seven-eighths
7⅛	seven and an eighth *or* seven and one-eighth
7.8	seven point eight
8.26	eight point two six

Exercise A

You will hear ten numbers. Circle the numbers that you hear.

1.	4/5	45	4 1/5	4.5
2.	2/8	208	2⅛	2.8
3.	2/5	25	2 1/5	2.5
4.	⅓	30	1⅓	1.3
5.	1/6	106	1 1/6	1.6
6.	¾	304	3¼	3.4
7.	⅞	78	7⅛	7.8
8.	⅔	23	2⅓	2.3
9.	3/5	35	3 1/5	3.5
10.	2/6	206	2 1/6	2.6

Exercise B

You will hear ten numbers. Write the numbers that you hear.

1. ______________________ 6. ______________________
2. ______________________ 7. ______________________
3. ______________________ 8. ______________________
4. ______________________ 9. ______________________
5. ______________________ 10. ______________________

⊞ Listening to and Taking Notes on Lectures Containing Numbers and Statistics

3 AMERICAN ATTITUDES TOWARD WORK

Vocabulary Related to Work

salary
income
wage
monetary rewards

advancement
promotion

meaningful work
job satisfaction

to get training
to learn a trade/skill

layoff
seniority
job security

to negotiate a contract
labor union

insurance
benefits
retirement
maternity/paternity/
   parental leave

regular hours
overtime hours
flexible hours

to pay time and a half

Additional Vocabulary

PRE-LECTURE DISCUSSION

A. Discuss the following questions as a class.

1. Which of these five characteristics is most important to you in your work (or future work)? Check one.

   _____ high income

   _____ job security

   _____ short work hours

   _____ important and meaningful work

   _____ chances for advancement

   Calculate the percentage of students in your class who chose each answer.

2. What characteristics are important to you in a job? Using the following scale, rank each characteristic from 1 to 4.

   1 very important
   2 important
   3 somewhat important
   4 not important

   _____ a. good health insurance and benefits

   _____ b. being able to work independently

   _____ c. recognition from coworkers and supervisors

   _____ d. contact with a lot of people

   _____ e. flexible hours

   _____ f. high income

   Calculate the percentage of students in your class who ranked each characteristic as very important (that is, a 1 on the scale).

B. Discuss the following questions in small groups.

1. Discuss your work experience. What jobs have you had? What did you like about them? What did you dislike? Why?

2. Describe your ideal job. What kind of work would you like to do? Why?

LISTEN AND NOTE

The lecture you will hear describes two polls that were conducted to find out what American workers considered important in their jobs. Take notes in the box on the following page. Focus on the main ideas: the two polls, their purpose, and their results. If you hear additional details about the results, you can try to note them, too.

poll
survey

to rank items
to (take a) poll/survey

respondent

random sample

margin of error

Additional
Vocabulary

2 Polls: Purpose:

Poll #1 (1990):   asked respondents to choose which of five items

was most important to them

ITEM	% SAYING ITEM WAS MOST IMPORTANT

Poll #2 (19   ): asked respondents to rank importance of each job characteristic

CHARACTERISTIC	% SAYING ITEM WAS VERY IMPORTANT
1.	
2.	
3.	
4.	
5.	
6.	
7.	
8.	
9.	
10.	
11.	
12.	
13.	
14.	
15.	
16.	

Conclusions:

USING YOUR NOTES

Use your notes to determine whether each statement is true or false. If you think the statement is false, be prepared to explain your reasons.

_____ a. These surveys confirmed the view that American workers value a high salary above all other job characteristics.

_____ b. These surveys confirmed the view that American workers value meaningful and interesting work highly.

_____ c. These surveys confirmed the view that American workers value shorter working hours and more vacation time above most other job characteristics.

_____ d. These polls were both conducted in 1990.

_____ e. Seventy-eight percent of the American workers responding to the second poll think that job security is the most important aspect of a job.

_____ f. Seventy-eight percent of the American workers responding to the second poll think that job security is very important in their work.

_____ g. Fifty-six percent of the American workers responding to the second poll think that high income is the most important aspect of a job.

COMPARING IDEAS

1. In small groups, compare notes. Do you have the same information? Did you note the same key words?

2. Compare your answers to the preceding questions with your classmates' answers. If you have different answers, check your notes and discuss your reasons for making your choices.

POST-LECTURE DISCUSSION

Discuss the following questions in small groups.

1. Do the findings of these polls sound right to you? Were you surprised about anything?

2. How do the findings compare to your own work experience? To your work expectations?

3. Read the following proverbs and quotes, and group them into two categories: those emphasizing the importance of work and those emphasizing the importance of leisure. Which proverb(s) or quote(s) do you agree with? Why?

> *The devil finds work for idle hands to do.* —**Proverb**

> *My father taught me to work, but not to love it. I never did like to work, and I don't deny it. I'd rather read, tell stories, crack jokes, talk, laugh—anything but work.*
> —**Abraham Lincoln, *sixteenth U.S. president (1809–1865)***

> *No other technique for the conduct of life attaches the individual so firmly to reality as laying emphasis on work; for his work at least gives him a secure place in a portion of reality, in the human community.*
> —**Sigmund Freud, *Austrian physician and psychoanalyst (1856–1939)***

> *All work and no play makes Jack a dull boy.* —**Proverb**

USING VOCABULARY

Use the vocabulary below to fill in the blanks in this lecture summary.

income   polls   monetary   value   satisfaction   meaningful   rank

The lecturer gives the results of two *(1)* _____ that were
conducted to find out about Americans' views about work. Though many people
think that a high *(2)* _____ would be of the greatest importance, the polls did not show this. Rather, the polls showed that workers
(3) _____ interesting and *(4)* _____
work above all. This does not mean that workers aren't interested in a higher
salary; it does mean that when asked to name the most important work characteristic, they didn't *(5)* _____ salary as top on their list. Of
course, when asked to name items that were very important to them,
(6) _____ issues as well as psychological issues were named.
It seems that many factors contribute to job *(7)* _____.

RETAINING VOCABULARY

Write at least five words from the lecture and discussion that you would like to
remember. Use each word in an example that will remind you of its meaning.

Example

poll: The polls showed that the majority of the people supported the president.

1. _____

_____

2. _____

_____

3. _____

_____

4. _____

_____

5. _____

_____

SPEAKING AND LISTENING ACTIVITY

Create a questionnaire to survey your classmates about their habits. You may
focus, for example, on habits related to studying, eating, or recreation.
Distribute the questionnaire to your classmates. Once you have collected and
complied the results, present them to your classmates in percentage form, and
have them take notes.

PRE-LECTURE READING AND DISCUSSION

Discuss the following questions in small groups.

1. What major technological breakthroughs have occurred in your lifetime? How have these breakthroughs affected your life and the lives of those around you?

2. If you were a CEO (chief executive officer) or a manager and wanted to encourage employee creativity, what would you do?

3. Read the following article from *Newsweek* magazine. What techniques do large corporations—such as Du Pont, Pfizer, 3M, and Bell Labs—use to encourage innovation?

The Houses of Invention

If the great inventions of the past were usually the work of an individual—a Gutenberg, an Edison, a Bell—then those of the twentieth century are increasingly the brainchildren of entire labs. In an age marked by an explosion of knowledge, argues Warren Bennis of the University of Southern California, "one is too small a number to produce greatness." Some solitary inventors notwithstanding, America's engines of invention are corporate labs. What makes a great one?

At Du Pont, it takes up to 250 ideas to generate one major, marketable new product. At Pfizer Inc., the yield is one new drug out of 100 possibilities. All of the ultimate losers suck up money before the winner pays off. Success therefore requires taking "monetary risks that would give most corporate finance officers a case of indigestion," says management guru Tom Peters.

At 3M, the rule is that 30 percent of sales must come from products less than four years old. And its scientists and engineers can spend up to 5 percent of company time on their own projects, without even telling man-agers what they're up to. Both policies send a clear signal that risk-taking is a core value. Du Pont researchers may pursue their blue-sky ideas one day a week. The idea is to be open to serendipity: every scientist makes mistakes, but only in a culture that encourages the exploration of the unknown do you get Teflon (when a Du Pont scientists working on Freon accidentally polymerized several gases into a white powder). "A universal characteristic of innovative companies is an open culture," says Rosabeth Moss Kanter of Harvard Business School.

In a corporate lab, the walls between chemists and physicists, metallurgists and mechanics are often lower than in academe. It was by throwing together physicists with metallurgists and chemists that Bell Labs wove together the diverse talents that invented the transistor. Says William Brinkman, vice president for physical-sciences research at Bell Labs, "We call it 'spontaneous teaming'—you see an interesting problem that another group is working on and you want to be part of it."

LISTEN AND NOTE

 You will hear a lecture that spans millions of years in technology, highlighting milestone events and their dates. Complete the following chart with the dates, technological breakthroughs, and locations (if mentioned).

to discover
to design
to invent
to devise
to develop

to patent

patent

innovation
breakthrough

Additional
Vocabulary

TECHNOLOGY: 1a. The application of science, esp. to industrial or

commercial objectives.   1b. The entire body of methods and materials

used to achieve such objectives.   2. Anthropol. The body of knowledge

available to a civilization that is of use in fashioning implements,

practicing manual arts and skills, and extracting or collecting materials.

DATE	TECHNOLOGICAL BREAKTHROUGH	LOCATION
2,400,000 B.C.	stone tools	
	ancestors began to control fire	
		Africa
		Japan
		Egypt
		Syria
		Greece
		Egypt
		China
		E. Europe
A.D.		Iran

Indust. Rev—tech. proceeding at incredible speed:

   e.g., tech esp. relevant to students

DATE	TECHNOLOGICAL BREAKTHROUGH

Conclusions:

COMPARING IDEAS

1. In small groups, compare notes. What information do you have that your classmates don't? What information do they have that you don't?

2. If you have missed information, request clarification from a classmate (e.g., "Excuse me, I didn't catch the date for the invention of photocopying. Do you have that in your notes?") or your teacher (e.g., "Excuse me. Could you repeat the date for the invention of photocopying?").

USING YOUR NOTES

1. You will hear eight statements about the lecture. Use your notes to decide whether each statement is true or false.

   a. _____   c. _____   e. _____   g. _____

   b. _____   d. _____   f. _____   h. _____

2. Write six statements about the information in the lecture. Include both true and false statements. Read them to your classmates and have them decide whether each statement is true or false.

   a. _____

   b. _____

   c. _____

   d. _____

   e. _____

   f. _____

POST-LECTURE DISCUSSION

Discuss the following questions in small groups.

1. The lecturer names several inventions that have occurred since the Industrial Revolution. Which of these inventions do you consider to be true milestones when examined from a perspective covering many thousands of years of technological advances?

2. Michio Kaku, a physicist, made the predictions below about future technology.

   Your watch or jewelry . . . may one day become an Internet node, capable of accessing the knowledge of an entire planet.

In the year 2020, your doctor may take a piece of your skin, and place it in a breadbox-sized device on the desk, which will spit out a CD with your name on it. This CD will be an "owner's manual" for your body with every single gene recorded.

Do you agree with Kaku's predictions? Why or why not? How do you imagine that technology will affect everyday lives in the year 2020?

3. Do you believe that some areas of technological research and development should be limited or prohibited? If so, which ones? Why?

DEFINING VOCABULARY

The following words and expressions were used in the lecture that you just heard. You may remember the contexts in which you heard them. You will hear an example of each word or expression in a new context. After listening, use context clues to write a definition for each word or expression.

1. objective _____

2. implement _____

3. turning point _____

4. to estimate _____

5. ancestor _____

6. to weave _____

7. to mine _____

8. to rely on _____

9. forerunner _____

RETAINING VOCABULARY

Write at least five words from the lecture, reading, and discussion that you would like to remember. Use each word in an example that will remind you of its meaning.

Example

patent: Inventors should patent their designs in order to protect their rights.

1. _____

_____

2. _____

_____

3. _____

_____

4. _____

_____

5. _____

_____

SPEAKING AND LISTENING ACTIVITY

What machine would you like to see invented? A machine to remember your dreams? An exercise machine that works while you sleep? Work with a partner to design an invention. Think about who might use the invention, what it would do, how it would work, why it would be helpful, and how much it should cost. Then design an advertisement for your invention. When you have finished, present your invention and your advertisement to your classmates. The following is an example.

WHO?	People with busy lives who don't enjoy cooking.
WHAT?	A machine with an extensive database of thousands of recipes, compartments for ingredients, and cooking and cleaning abilities.
HOW?	1. Program in the foods that are in the kitchen.
	2. The IGM provides a selection of possible recipes.
	3. Choose a recipe and place each ingredient in a separate compartment.
	4. The IGM cooks the dish and signals when the food is ready.
	5. The IGM cleans itself automatically.
WHY?	It can save people time and energy, so they have more time to do the things they enjoy!
PRICE:	$5,000

LECTURE 5 IMMIGRATION TO THE UNITED STATES

PRE-LECTURE READING AND DISCUSSION

Vocabulary Related to Immigration

to immigrate
to emigrate

ancestry
ancestor

descendant

ethnicity
ethnic diversity

to blend in
to assimilate

to retain one's identity

to seek refuge/asylum

to flee
to escape

persecution
oppression

melting pot

Additional Vocabulary

Discuss the following questions in small groups.

1. The following excerpt is from a poem which is inscribed on the base of the Statue of Liberty. It was written by Emma Lazarus in 1883 to express her belief that the Statue of Liberty could be the "Mother of Exiles" and that it would welcome all to its shores, especially the tired, the poor, the "huddled masses yearning to breathe free," the "wretched refuse"—that is, it would welcome those whom other countries didn't want.

   Read the excerpt. Then discuss the questions that follow.

   > *Give me your tired, your poor,*
   > *Your huddled masses yearning to breathe free,*
   > *The wretched refuse of your teeming shore.*
   > *Send these, the homeless, tempest-tost to me,*
   > *I lift my lamp beside the golden door!*

   a. Do you believe that the United States has lived up to the ideals in the poem? If so, how? If not, why not?
   b. Do you believe it is possible to live up to the ideals in the poem? Why or why not?

2. If you are an immigrant, why did you immigrate? What has your experience as an immigrant been like? If you are not an immigrant, would you consider immigrating? If so, under what circumstances?

3. Consider your native country or a country you know well. Do many people immigrate there? Where do the immigrants typically come from? Has immigration had any effects on the country? If so, what are they?

4. Consider your native country or a country you know well. Do many people emigrate from there? Where do the emigrants typically go? Has emigration had any effects on the country? If so, what are they?

LISTEN AND NOTE

 You will hear a lecture that consists of statistics about immigration from particular continents for the years 1820 to 1995, as well as from individual countries for 1995. Complete the chart with the numbers that you hear.

U.S. — land of immigrants

only   — true Americans

U.S. — melting pot?   or   stew?

	1820-1995		1995	
LOCATIONS	TOTAL #	%	TOTAL #	%
From all countries				
From continents				
Europe				
Asia				
Americas				
Africa				
Oceania				
From individual countries				
Mexico				
Philippines				
Vietnam				
Korea				
Cuba				
Dominican Republic				
Ukraine				
Canada				
India				
China (incl. Taiwan)				

COMPARING IDEAS

1. In small groups, compare notes. What information do you have that your classmates don't? What information do they have that you don't?

2. If you missed information, request clarification from a classmate (e.g., "Excuse me, I didn't catch the number of immigrants coming from India in 1995. Do you have that in your notes?") or your teacher (e.g., "Excuse me. Could you repeat the statistics for India, please?").

USING YOUR NOTES

1. Which pie chart best shows the breakdown of immigration by continent from 1820 to 1995?

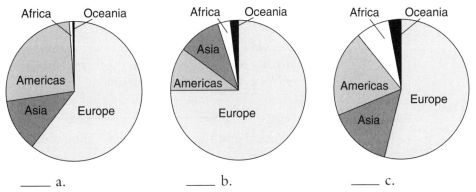

_____ a.   _____ b.   _____ c.

2. Draw a pie chart showing the breakdown of immigration by continent in 1995.

3. You will hear fifteen statements about immigration statistics. Listen to each statement. Use your notes to decide whether each statement is true or false.

a. _____   d. _____   g. _____   j. _____   m. _____

b. _____   e. _____   h. _____   k. _____   n. _____

c. _____   f. _____   i. _____   l. _____   o. _____

4. Write five statements about the immigration statistics that you just heard. Include both true and false statements. Read them to your classmates. Have them decide whether each statement is true or false.

a. _____

b. _____

c. _____

d. _____

e. _____

POST-LECTURE DISCUSSION

Discuss the following questions in small groups.

1. What did you find out from these statistics that you didn't know or expect?
2. Do you think the United States is more of a "melting pot" or a "stew"? Why? Which do you think it should be? What are the advantages of each one? The disadvantages?

USING VOCABULARY

 Before reading the following exercise, listen to a story that was originally told by the descendant of an immigrant. After listening, based on the information that you heard, fill in the blanks with words from the vocabulary list. (You may change the verb forms and tenses.)

to immigrate	to emigrate	ancestors
melting pot	descendants	to retain their ethnic identity
to blend in	ethnic diversity	

My *(1)* _____ came from Eastern Europe, primarily Poland and the former Soviet Union. Some of them *(2)* _____ to the United States because they longed for opportunities and adventures; others *(3)* _____ from their homeland because of persecution. They came to New York with the hopes that this port city with its great *(4)* _____ would allow them to *(5)* _____ with the crowds without being too noticeable. However, New York, the supposed *(6)* _____ of cultures, was in reality a stew. The new immigrants mixed with the others but definitely *(7)* _____. I don't think they ever completely adjusted to their new lives.

RETAINING VOCABULARY

Write at least five words from the lecture, poem, and discussion that you would like to remember. Use each word in an example that will remind you of its meaning.

Example

flee: The people had to flee their homes without their belongings because of the quickly spreading fire.

1. _____

_____

2. _____
   _____
3. _____
   _____
4. _____
   _____
5. _____
   _____

SPEAKING AND LISTENING ACTIVITY

Research recent immigration to and emigration from your native country (or a country of your choice). Present your findings to your classmates using pie charts for visual support. Speculate about some reasons for and effects of that immigration.

5

LISTENING FOR ORGANIZATION IN LECTURES

▷ Goals

- Learn about the different organizational plans used by lecturers
- Learn about the cues that signal these organizational plans
- Recognize the relationship between ideas in a lecture
- Recognize introductions and conclusions
- Recognize tangential information

▣ Why Listen for Organization?

The organization of a lecture is not like the organization of a piece of writing. As discussed in Unit 1, spoken language allows for much more paraphrase, repetition, and tangential information. Because spoken language is temporal (i.e., it does not last long in time), organization is much more flexible. A speaker may raise a topic, go off on a tangent or discuss a related topic, and finally return to the topic. Also, a speaker signals new ideas and emphasizes ideas by using linguistic means, paralinguistic means (e.g., intonation), or body language (e.g., leaning forward).

When listening to a lecture, the listener must first try to figure out the lecturer's goals. For example, does the lecturer want the listener to understand a definition? Visualize how something looks? Understand how something works? Understand a concept? Generally, a lecturer organizes his or her ideas in some manner in order to communicate them. Although lecturers vary in the degree that they "stick to an outline," even a lecturer who "talks off the top of his or her head" has an organizational plan.

Why listen for organization? Research has shown that it is easier to retain interrelated information than isolated facts. By recognizing the organization of a lecture, the listener is better able to relate facts to each other. Specifically, the listener is better able to:

- understand the lecturer's goals

- make predictions about where the lecture is heading

- retain information

Using Introductions to Recognize Lecture Focus and Direction

Most lecturers begin with some sort of introductory cues or remarks. Listeners need to recognize when the speaker has finished the introduction and begun the body of the lecture, which contains the key points.

Lecturers start their lectures in different ways. Some provide background information that leads up to their topic. Others begin with a few personal stories or comments about a shared experience to relax the audience. Some lecturers give overviews of their whole lecture plan and explicitly state their goals. Others give general statements about a topic.

Most often, the introduction is a good time for the listener to *listen* (rather than rush to note) in order to get a good idea of what the lecturer's goals are. This way, the listener has a framework or plan for predicting what will be discussed in the lecture.

EXAMPLES OF CUES TO RECOGNIZING INTRODUCTIONS

1. Sentences giving an explicit overview of the lecture:

   I'd like to do two things. The first is to define X. The second is to give a few examples of X.

2. Sentences indicating a lecture's general focus:

   We're going to be talking about X today.

3. Sentences or rhetorical questions referring to a continuation of a previous lecture:

   Last time we were talking about X.
   Where did we leave off yesterday?

Exercise

 You will hear the beginnings of seven different lectures. First, read the question about each excerpt. Then listen to the excerpt. After listening, circle the letter of the best answer.

Example

This lecture will be about
a. the physical and emotional benefits and drawbacks of being an employed woman or a housewife.
b. the reactions of the world to employed women and housewives.
c. the effects of the women's liberation movement.
d. the working habits of women in the United States.

The lecturer said:

> What I would like to focus on in this lecture are some of the factors a woman might want to take into account when deciding whether to enter the job market or not . . . A major question would be which one is emotionally and physically more beneficial . . .

Other ideas were mentioned in the introduction, but this statement addresses the focus of the lecture. It indicates that the body of the lecture will be about the physical and emotional benefits and drawbacks of being an employed woman or a housewife. Therefore, the best answer is (a).

1. This lecture will be about
   a. the many things that we eat which are harmful to us.
   b. people's attitudes toward new findings about the side effects of certain foods.
   c. a study that showed the effect of alcohol on the fetus.
   d. the type of foods that pregnant women should not eat.

2. This lecture will be about
   a. the basic structure of all ecosystems.[1]
   b. particular ecosystems and their characteristics.
   c. the differences between ecosystems.
   d. human influences on ecosystems.

3. This lecture will be about
   a. the reasons for American marriage and divorce patterns.
   b. American marriage and divorce patterns over a period of time.
   c. what non-Americans think of American marriage and divorce patterns.
   d. the effects of American marriage and divorce patterns.

4. This lecture will be about
   a. prenatal[2] development.
   b. physical growth from birth to adolescence.
   c. emotional and physical growth from birth to adolescence.
   d. a and b.
   e. a, b, and c.

---

[1] **ecosystem:** a system involving a relationship between organisms and the environment

[2] **prenatal:** relating to the period before birth

5. This lecture will be about (circle as many as are correct)
   a. the university's role in meeting Asian-American student needs.
   b. a history of Asian immigration to the United States.
   c. the cultural and psychological characteristics of Asian-Americans in the United States
   d. the present status of Asian-Americans in the United States.

6. This lecture will be about (circle as many as are correct)
   a. foreign policy in Latin America.
   b. politics.
   c. doing library-based research.
   d. the process of looking for information.

7. The primary purpose of this lecture on ecology[3] will be to give students
   a. a *reasoned* and *emotional* approach to the relationship between the human species and its environment.
   b. a *reasoned* approach to the relationship between the human species and its environment.
   c. general scientific concepts.
   d. an *emotional* approach to the relationship between the human species and its environment.

Recognizing and Comprehending Conclusions

Some lecturers end their lectures abruptly. They may say something such as, "Oh! Time's up. I'll continue tomorrow." However, many lecturers use conclusions to finalize their lectures. This might involve reviewing the lecture's key points, making general statements that tie different aspects of the topic together, or discussing the topic's consequences. Conclusions that involve a review or a generalization provide the listeners with a chance to check whether their notes reflect what the lecturer thought was important.

EXAMPLES OF CUES TO RECOGNIZING CONCLUSIONS

1. Words signaling a forthcoming summary, logical conclusion, or ending:

   So, . . .
   Therefore, . . .
   Thus, . . .
   Consequently, . . .
   In sum, . . .
   In conclusion, . . .

2. Words or phrases that tie together previously stated ideas:

   For (all of) these reasons, . . .
   These examples (serve to) show . . .

---

[3] **ecology:** the science that deals with the interrelationships between organisms and their environment

Organizational Plans within Lectures

Rule 7 of the DOs and DON'Ts for improving lecture comprehension and note-taking in Unit 3 was the following:

> DON'T lose sight of the forest for the trees. (Don't listen for details before getting the larger picture.)
>
> DO listen for the lecturer's main points and for the general organizational framework.

The term *general organizational framework* refers to the *macro*structure, the overall organizational plan, of the lecture.

When looking at the organization of lectures, it is important to distinguish between the *macro*structure of the lecture and the *micro*structure of the lecture. The macrostructure refers to the organizational plan for the whole lecture. For example, the purpose of the whole lecture is to make a generalization and support that generalization, or the purpose of the whole lecture is to show the cause-and-effect relationship between two events. The microstructure refers to organization within the macrostructure, that is, the organization of smaller units within the lecture. For example, the lecturer's main purpose may be to make a generalization and support that generalization. However, in order to do so, the lecturer may define terms, provide examples, or describe processes.

In a lecture, one or more of the following organizational plans may be used at a macrostructure or a microstructure level:

> Defining a Term
> Listing Subtopics
> Describing a Causal Relationship
> Exemplifying a Topic
> Describing a Process or Sequence of Events
> Classifying Subtopics
> Describing Characteristics
> Comparing and Contrasting
> Making a Generalization and Providing Evidence

These plans are not mutually exclusive; that is, they can exist together. For example, a lecturer may state that "there has been little research on the effects of smoke from a nuclear explosion," and follow this up with a description of the research that has been done on this topic from 1980 up until the present. This lecturer would then be using two organizational plans: (1) making a generalization and providing evidence and (2) describing a sequence of events.

How does a listener recognize these organizational plans? Each of these plans will be examined in more detail in the pages that follow.

Defining a Term

In this case, the lecturer's goal is to define a term. A *simple definition* can take the form of a single statement, such as "The biosphere is simply that region of the earth in which organisms can exist." An *extended definition* expands upon the ideas in the simple definition by, for example, explaining the term in more detail. An extended definition might even be a whole lecture!

Notes from a lecture using this pattern might look like this:

Biosphere — region of earth in which organisms can exist

    — extends ↑ to ~ 20,000 ft. altitude

    — " " ↓ to bottom of ocean

    — " " inwards to limit of 100 ft.

When the lecturer gives a definition, the listener's task is to note the key words or the ideas that make up the definition.

EXAMPLES OF CUES TO RECOGNIZING DEFINITIONS

1. Rhetorical questions referring back to a term requiring a definition or explanation:

    What do I mean by X?
    How can we define X?

2. Words or phrases signaling a definition or explanation:

    (Now,) X means (is the word for) . . .
    By X, I mean (meant, referred to) . . .
    When I used X, I meant (was referring to) . . .

3. Terms written on the board and explained:

biotic

4. Terms followed by appositives (noun phrase definitions):

    These are the biotic components . . . *the living components* . . .

5. Stress, intonation, and pauses used with appositives:

Note the stress on the words *biotic* and *living*, which emphasize their importance. Note the pause between *biotic components* and *the living components*. Finally, note the repetition of the stress pattern for *the biotic components* and *the living components*. All of the paralinguistic features of language (stress, intonation, pauses) carry meaning.

Exercise A

 Listen for the appositive in each of the following excerpts. Write the meaning of each word.

Example

abiotic: nonbiological

1. entity _____
2. hearth _____
3. herbivores _____
4. terminology _____

Exercise B

 Listen to each of the following lecture excerpts. While listening, write the definition of each term.

Example

In this excerpt from a lecture on the costs or benefits of employment to women, the lecturer defines a term.

emotional strength: the degree of psych. distress to which s.o. reacts to life crisis

1. In this excerpt from a lecture on family systems, the lecturer defines two contrasting terms.

    a. exogamy _____

    b. endogamy _____

2. In this excerpt, also from a lecture on family systems, the lecturer again defines two contrasting terms.

    a. emic _____

    b. etic _____

3. In this excerpt from a lecture on ecology, the lecturer names the term and follows it with a definition. Note the cue "by metabolism, I mean . . . "

    metabolism _____

4. In this excerpt from a lecture on ecology, the lecturer names the term and follows it with a definition. Note the cue "now that means . . . "

    irritability _____

5. In this excerpt from a lecture on ecology, the lecturer defines *life* by giving the criteria for judging life. The lecturer ends by tying the information together into a simple definition.

    life _____

    _____

    _____

For additional practice recognizing and noting definitions (as a major or minor organizational pattern in a lecture), listen to any of the following lectures:

Lecture 6   How to Deal with Stress (page 83)
Lecture 7   Acid Rain (page 91)
Lecture 10   Pheromones (page 116)
Lecture 11   The Near Side of the Moon (page 124)
Lecture 16   Earthquakes: Can They Be Predicted? (page 168)
Lecture 17   Hall's Classification of Cultures (page 177)

Listing Subtopics

In this case, the lecturer's goal is to break a topic down by listing or enumerating a number of features of the topic. For example, in a lecture on Amnesty International, a human rights organization, the lecturer lists eight principles upon which the group's work is based.

Notes from this lecture might look like this:

---

8 Principles Underlying Amnesty International's Work

   1. limited field of authority

      — limits work to political imprisonment, torture, execution

   2. focus on individual prisoner

      — does not work in abstract

      — seeks contact w/ prisoners & families

  etc.

Note that each numbered item is related to the larger heading in the same way as the other numbered items. That is, they are all underlying principles of Amnesty International's work.

EXAMPLES OF CUES TO RECOGNIZING LISTS

1. Numbers indicating listed items:

   The first (second, etc.) point is . . .
   Number one (two, etc.) . . .
   First (second, etc.) of all . . .

2. Stress emphasizing numbers:

   The first principle is . . .

3. Phrases or sentences signaling a list of forthcoming items:

   There are eight principles which underlie Amnesty International's work.
   Stress can be reduced in a number of ways.

Exercise

 You will hear four lecture excerpts that list information. First, read the information about each excerpt. Then, while listening to the excerpt, take notes in the spaces provided.

Example

Excerpt from a lecture on the costs or benefits of employment to women.

heading

list

How to Judge Psych. Distress?
1. how much anxiety
2. " " irritability
3. " " somatic (bodily/complaints)
4. " " depression
5. " " problems w/ thinking & concentrating

1. Excerpt from a lecture on ecology.

   VOCABULARY
   ecosystem: a system involving a relationship between organisms and the environment
   nutrient: an ingredient in food that nourishes (i.e., keeps an organism alive)

heading

list

Essential Abiotic Factors for Life in Ecosystem—
1.
2.
3.
4.

2. Excerpt from a lecture on eight steps of topic analysis for library research.

heading

list

While Surveying Topic & Clarifying Terms
1.
2.

3. Excerpt from a lecture on human development.

VOCABULARY
premature: occurring before the expected time
fetus: an unborn being (in humans, from the ninth week to birth)
womb: the place in the mother's body where the fetus develops
incubator: a machine providing an ideal environment for the development of premature babies
to monitor: to watch carefully; to check regularly
kid: (informal) a child

heading

list

What Needs to Be Done to Keep a Premature Kid Alive?
1.
2.

4. Excerpt from a lecture on human development.

VOCABULARY
fetal: relating to the fetus
embryo: an organism in the earliest stages of development, before it becomes a fetus
cell: the smallest unit of an organism that can function independently

heading

list

3 Things That Happen during the Prenatal Period
1.
2.
3.

For additional practice recognizing and noting listed items (as a major or minor organizational pattern in a lecture), listen to any of the following lectures:

Lecture 3	American Attitudes toward Work (page 34)
Lecture 6	How to Deal with Stress (page 83)
Lecture 9	Amnesty International (page 107)
Lecture 13	Voter Turnout in the United States (page 140)

⊞ Describing a Causal Relationship

In this case, the lecturer's goal is to describe a relationship between events in which one event leads to (or may or should lead to) one or more events.

This pattern might include a combination of the following:

- a description of a problem or the circumstances surrounding an event
- the causes of, or reasons for, the problem or circumstances
- the effects of the problem or circumstances
- the solution to a problem

Notes from a lecture using this pattern might look like this:

Acid Rain
— destroys structures
— harms environment
Causes?
— auto emissions
— industrial emissions
Solutions?
— control emissions
BUT $$

EXAMPLES OF CUES TO RECOGNIZING CAUSAL RELATIONSHIPS

1. Words and phrases signaling a causal relationship:

   Due to the fact that . . .
   Because of . . .
   Since . . .
   Conditional Sentences: If . . . , (then) . . .
   (Now) this is due to . . .
   It has nothing to do with X, but rather . . .
   . . . and the reason for this is . . .

2. Words or phrases signaling the effect of a previously stated event:

   Thus, . . .
   Therefore, . . .
   Consequently, . . .
   For these reasons, . . .

3. Rhetorical questions signaling a discussion of the cause of a previously stated event:

   > How can we explain this?
   > How did we get to this point?
   > Why is this the case?

4. Rhetorical questions signaling a discussion of the solution to a previously stated problem:

   > What can be done about this?
   > How can we solve this?

Exercise

 You will hear four lecture excerpts that describe causal relationships. First, read the information about each excerpt. Then, while listening, take notes in the spaces provided.

Example

Excerpt from a lecture on eight steps of topic analysis for library research.

event   7th Step — See Topic in Broadest Way
— Think about academic disciplines related to topic
reason   Why? — different academic subjects look at topic from
different vantage pts.

1. Excerpt from a lecture on marriage and divorce trends in the United States. (Note the cue "because" in "people get married much more quickly than they would have in normal times *because* . . . ")

event   1940 — Close to Begin of WW II (Pre-War)
↓
effect
cause   Why?

2. Excerpt from a lecture on marriage and divorce trends in the United States. Note the cue "and we can probably draw some conclusions about what separations do for marriages."

event	1945 — Men Come Home fr. War
	↓
effect	
cause	Why?

3. Excerpt from a lecture on Asian-Pacific immigration to the United States. (Note the cue "*so* the people started coming.")

cause	1965 — U.S. Changes Immigration Law
	(previously # of Asians small because quota ~ 100 people per country/yr)
	↓
effect	

4. Excerpt from a lecture on acid rain. (Note the cue, "What can we do?")

problem	Acid Rain ↑ w/Industrialization
solution	Solutions?
problem w/solution	BUT

For additional practice recognizing and noting causal relationships (as a major or minor organizational pattern in a lecture), listen to any of the following lectures:

Lecture 7   Acid Rain (page 91)
Lecture 13   Voter Turnout in the United States (page 140)
Lecture 16   Earthquakes: Can They Be Predicted? (page 168)

Exemplifying a Topic

In this case, the goal of the lecturer is to clarify the topic by giving examples. For instance, in a lecture on archaeology, the lecturer talks about estimating dates by reading tree rings. He gives examples of how the rings might look under different conditions.

Notes from a lecture using this pattern might look like this:

Archaeological Dating Methods

Tree-ring dating (dendrochronology)

— every yr., trees grow new layer

— create series of concentric rings

— layer varies with climatic changes

e.g., spring — pale ring

e.g., drought — thin ring

— archaeologists start from known climatic changes and count back

EXAMPLES OF CUES TO RECOGNIZING EXAMPLES

1. Phrases signaling an example:

   For example, . . .
   For instance, . . .
   To illustrate, . . .
   In this case, . . .
   Let's say, . . .
   Take something like this . . .

2. Phrases or sentences emphasizing the application of a concept:

   In order to see this more clearly, . . .
   In more concrete terms, . . .
   Let's look at how this applies in the real world.

3. Rhetorical questions signaling an example:

   Where can we find/see this?
   How does this show up in the real world?

Exercise

 You will hear four lecture excerpts that include examples. First, read the information about each excerpt. Then, while listening to the excerpt, take notes in the spaces provided.

Example

Excerpt from a lecture on ecology.

heading — Level of Light That Plants Tolerate Varies Greatly
examples — e.g., shade plants — need low light; die in sun
other plants — sit in sun all day
not just temp. — also light intensity

1. Excerpt from a lecture on ecology.

heading — W/Cold-Blooded Animals, Chem. Reactions Depend on Temp. of Environ.
examples — e.g.,

2. Excerpt from a lecture on family systems.

heading — Terms for "Cousin" Vary in Diff. Languages
examples — e.g.,

3. Excerpt from a lecture on eight steps of topic analysis for library research.

heading — 2nd Step — Break Topic into Subtopics
examples — e.g.,

4. Excerpt from a lecture on family systems.

> VOCABULARY
> **boundary**: something that indicates a limit
> **caste system**: a social system that divides society into groups that are restricted in terms of occupation and marriage

heading	Endogamy Sometimes in Marriage Patterns
definition	
examples	e.g.,

For additional practice recognizing and noting examples (as a major or minor organizational pattern in a lecture), listen to any of the following lectures:

Lecture 8   Archaeological Dating Methods (page 98)
Lecture 10   Pheromones (page 116)
Lecture 13   Voter Turnout in the United States (page 140)
Lecture 14   How to Look at Art (page 149)
Lecture 15   Paging Robodoc: Robots in Medicine (page 158)
Lecture 17   Hall's Classification of Cultures (page 177)

Describing a Process or Sequence of Events

In this case, the lecturer's goal is to demonstrate how something happens (or happened) by organizing information according to a process or sequence of events.

Notes from a lecture organized as a process might look like this:

5 Steps in Processing Film	
— Develop	— makes images visible
— Rinse	— stops development
— Fix	— removes unused light-sensitive silver bromide
	— hardens photosensitive material for safe handling
— Wash	— removes dissolved chemicals from print or film
— Dry	

Notes from a lecture organized as a sequence of events might look like this:

Research on Smoke as Effect of Nuclear War
— to 1982, smoke barely mentioned in literature
— '82 — Crutzen & Birks calculated effect of 100,000,000s tons
smoke on earth
— found smoke would change phys. properties of Earth's
atmosphere
— calc. based only on burning forests
— post-'82 — Turco, Sagan & others added effects of burning cities
to calc.

CUES FOR RECOGNIZING A PROCESS OR SEQUENCE OF EVENT

1. Time expressions signaling a sequence of events or steps in a process:

   First (Second, etc.), . . .
   Next (Then, Subsequently, Later, After that, etc.), . . .
   Prior to (Previously, Before that, etc.), . . .
   In 1965 (In the first century, etc.), . . .

2. Phrases or sentences signaling a sequence of events or steps in a process:

   In order to arrive at this point, we had to . . .
   We can trace the development . . .

   Let's look at
   $\begin{cases} \text{how this came about.} \\ \text{where this comes from.} \\ \text{how to X.} \\ \text{(the steps involved in) this process.} \end{cases}$

3. Rhetorical questions signaling a description of a process or sequence of events:

   Where did this idea come from?
   How can we do this?
   How did this come about?

Exercise

 You will hear four lecture excerpts that include descriptions of processes or sequences of events. First, read the information about each excerpt. Then, while listening to the excerpts, take notes in the spaces provided.

Example

Excerpt from a lecture by Carl Sagan on global community.

heading	All Humans Come from Same Area — E. Africa
sequence	species Homo sapiens began there — a few 100,000 yrs. ago
	human family " " " " " million " "
	initially — small group— family members
	— wandering
	— following game
	— #s — few
	— powers — feeble
	intervening yrs. — humans expanded to every continent
	— incl. oceans & space!
now	— 5.6 bill. humans
	— awesome powers!

1. Excerpt from a lecture on human development.

   VOCABULARY
   embryo: an organism in the earliest stages of development, before it becomes a fetus
   blood vessels: veins through which blood flows

heading	Embryonic Period
sequence	1st mo.
	by end of 1st mo.
	2nd mo.

2. Excerpt from a lecture on the spread of the plague.

VOCABULARY
plague: a deadly disease that spreads quickly
epidemic: many cases of a disease that spreads quickly
pandemic: an epidemic spread over a very wide area
medieval times: A.D. 1000-1500, the Middle Ages
outbreak: a sudden appearance of a disease

3 Great Pandemics of Plague in Recorded History
1st
2nd
3rd

3. Excerpt from a lecture on library research.

First 8 Steps for Library Research (continued)
1. survey topic (look for broadest discussion)
and clarify unfamiliar terms
2. break topic into simple subtopics
3. look for types of info. needed to research subject
4.
5.
6.

4. Excerpt from a lecture on social psychology.

> VOCABULARY
> **norm**: an accepted or expected standard of behavior or thinking among a given group of people

heading	Rituals — set or series of actions taking place in certain order — form norm
sequence	e.g., Argyle (British psychol.) identified steps in "new neighbor ritual"
	(when new family moves into neighborhood)
	1.
	2.
	3.
	4.
	5.
	6.
	7.
conclusion	Knowledge of rituals makes us skillful in given society

For additional practice recognizing and noting processes or sequences (as a major or minor organizational pattern in a lecture), listen to any of the following lectures:

Lecture 4   Milestones in Technology (page 38)
Lecture 5   Immigration to the United States (page 43)
Lecture 8   Archaeological Dating Methods (page 98)
Lecture 12   Drink Your Green Tea! (page 132)
Lecture 15   Paging Robodoc: Robots in Medicine (page 158)
Lecture 16   Earthquakes: Can They Be Predicted? (page 168)

Classifying Subtopics

In this case, the lecturer's goal is to make a topic more manageable by creating classifications in which to organize the information from the larger topic.

A *classification* provides headings so that information can be grouped together based on similar characteristics. For example, a geologist may present a lecture on rocks by talking about the three different kinds of rocks: igneous rocks, sedimentary rocks, and metamorphic rocks. If the lecture compared the types while describing them, this would be a combination of a classification organizational plan and a comparison/contrast organizational plan.

Notes from a lecture presenting a classification might look like this:

Edward Hall's Classification of Cultures
Low-Context Cultures
— more attention given to message or event than to context of event
i.e., message/event has meaning in itself
e.g., German, Swiss cultures
High-Context Cultures
— more attention paid to context of message or event than to message itself
i.e., more important who you are, your family connections, than words
e.g., Arab, Greek cultures

Alternatively, these notes might be organized in columns:

Edward Hall's Classification of Cultures	
Low-Context Cultures	High-Context Cultures
— more attention given to messages or event than to context of event	— more attention paid to context of message or event than to message itself
i.e., message/event has meaning in itself	i.e., more important who you are, your family connections, than words
e.g., German, Swiss cultures	e.g., Arab, Greek cultures

EXAMPLES OF CUES TO RECOGNIZING CLASSIFICATIONS

1. Phrases indicating categories:

$$X \text{ can be} \begin{cases} \text{divided} \\ \text{subdivided} \\ \text{broken down} \\ \text{classified} \end{cases} \text{into 2 (3, 4, etc.)} \begin{cases} \text{groups.} \\ \text{schools of thought.} \\ \text{divisions.} \\ \text{categories.} \\ \text{classifications.} \end{cases}$$

$$\text{There are 2 (3, 4, etc.)} \begin{cases} \text{types of} \\ \text{schools of thought about} \\ \text{divisions of} \\ \text{classifications of} \end{cases} X.$$

2. Rhetorical questions signaling classifications:

What types of X are there?
How can X be classified/categorized?

Exercise

 You will hear four lecture excerpts that include classifications. First, read the information about each excerpt. Then, while listening to the excerpts, take notes in the spaces provided.

Example

Excerpt from a lecture on family systems.

heading

classifications

Types of Households	
— patrilocal	— couple lives w/ husband's father
— virilocal	— couple lives w/ husband's family — not father
— matrilocal	— " " " " wife's mother
— uxorilocal	— " " " " wife's family — not mother
— avunculocal	— " " " " husband's mother's brother
— neolocal	— " " " independently

1. Excerpt from a lecture on human development.

    VOCABULARY
    womb: the place in the mother's body where the fetus develops
    conception: the forming of an embryo; the beginning of pregnancy

heading

classifications

3 Periods of Development in Womb
—
—
—

2. Excerpt from a lecture on eight steps to topic analysis for library research.

heading

classifications

3rd Step — Look for Types of Info. Needed to Research Subject
—
—

3. Excerpt from a lecture on marriage systems.

VOCABULARY
spouse: a husband or wife

heading	Two Kinds of Polygamy (Plural Spouses)
classifications	&
subclassifications	

4. Excerpt from a lecture on family systems.

VOCABULARY
kin: relatives
compensation: payment for a service or loss

term	Marriage Payment — Most Common in Arranged Marriages
definition	— Alliance betw. families to compensate other for work & reproductive
	potential
heading	Types of payments:
classifications	—
	—
	—

For additional practice recognizing and noting items in a classification (as a major or minor organizational pattern in a lecture), listen to any of the following lectures:

▣ Describing Characteristics

In this case, the lecturer's goal is to describe an object or living thing through its characteristics. In particular, the lecturer focuses on the object's physical qualities and setting.

Notes from a lecture using this pattern might look like this:

Blue Whales		
Size	— fully grown — 100 ft.	
	— newborn calves — 23 ft.	
Weight	— fully grown — 130 tons	
	— newborn — 2 tons	
Color	— bluish gray	

EXAMPLES OF CUES TO RECOGNIZING DESCRIPTIONS

1. Phrases or sentences describing an object's characteristics:

   Concerning X's appearance, . . .
   Let's look at X's physical makeup.
   X is made up of . . .
   The layout of X is . . .

2. Phrases referring to sensory perception:

   $$X \begin{Bmatrix} \text{looks} \\ \text{acts} \\ \text{feels} \\ \text{smells} \\ \text{sounds} \\ \text{tastes} \end{Bmatrix} \text{like} \ldots$$

   If we were to visit (see, draw, examine, etc.) X, we would see . . .

3. Analogies:

   X is spiderlike (humanlike, etc.).

4. Prepositions of place (and other terms) describing position:

above	under	adjacent to
below	next to	across from
on	diagonal(ly)	on the right/left
in	vertical(ly)	in the back/front/center
over	horizontal(ly)	in the foreground/background

5. Rhetorical questions preceding descriptions:

   What does X look (act, feel, etc.) like?

Exercise

 You will hear three lecture excerpts that include descriptions. The items to be described are noted for you. First, read the information about each excerpt. Then, while listening to the excerpts, write as many descriptive details as you can.

Example

Excerpt from an anthropology lecture describing a typical wife's house in a Masai village.

item	Wife's House in Masai Village
description	— 2 beds (for ♀ & ♂)
	not husband, for guests, adult sons
	built on platforms w/cowhide on top
	— wood fire in middle of house
	— no windows, just airholes nr. beds ∴ SMOKY
	— 25' long x 15' wide
	— goats/sheep also in house

1. Excerpt from a lecture on ecology.

   VOCABULARY
   shrub: a bush; a woody plant

item	Typical Deciduous Woodland
description	

2. Excerpt from a lecture on human development.

   VOCABULARY
   embryo: an organism in the earliest stage of development, before it becomes a fetus
   limb: an arm or leg

item	2nd Month of Embryo Development
description	

3. Excerpt from the same lecture on human development.

> VOCABULARY
> **fetus:** an unborn being (in humans, from the ninth week to birth)
> **fetal:** relating to the fetus

item

description

4th — 5th Month of Fetal Development —

For additional practice recognizing and noting descriptions (as a major or minor organizational pattern in a lecture), listen to any of the following lectures:

Lecture 11   The Near Surface of the Moon (page 124)
Lecture 14   How to Look at Art (page 149)
Lecture 15   Paging Robodoc: Robots in Medicine (page 158)

⊞ Comparing and Contrasting

In this case, the lecturer's goal is to show the similarities and differences between items. The lecturer may compare and contrast the items by first talking about each item individually and then comparing and contrasting them. Notes from a lecture using this pattern might look like this:

Differences betw. Listening to Lecture and Everyday Listening	
Listening to Lecture	
Speaker/listener interaction:	generally unidirectional
	listener — no control over direction
	of lecture
Expectations of listener:	note & retain info. for later use
Everyday Listening Situation	
Interaction:	generally interactive
	listener can ask for clarification,
	repetition, even change topic
Expectations of listener:	make immed. response
∴ Differences in interaction and expectations	

The lecturer may also compare and contrast the items point by point. Notes from a lecture using this pattern might look like this:

Differences betw. Listening to Lecture and Everyday Listening		
	LISTENING TO LECTURE	EVERYDAY LISTENING
SPEAKER/	generally unidirectional	generally interactive
LISTENER	listener has no control	listener can ask for
INTERACTION	over direction of	clarification, repetition,
	lecture	or even change topic
EXPECTATIONS	note and retain info.	make immediate response
OF LISTENER:	for later use	

Regardless of the lecturer's style of speaking, the note-taker's goals should be to visually represent the differences and similarities between the items. Notice that in the notes just shown, it is very easy to glance down the left-hand margin and see the *areas* of comparison and contrast. In this way, the comparison/contrast is not simply a collection of unrelated similarities and differences; rather, the similarities and differences are grouped according to topic. This is not always possible when taking notes, but it is very helpful to do when revising or rewriting notes.

EXAMPLES OF CUES TO RECOGNIZING COMPARISONS AND CONTRASTS

1. Words and phrases indicating a contrast between preceding and following information:

   But . . .
   However, . . .
   On the other hand, . . .
   On the contrary, . . .
   Conversely, . . .

2. Words and phrases indicating a similarity between preceding and following information:

   Similarly, . . .
   Likewise, . . .
   Along the same lines, . . .
   In the same fashion/manner, . . .
   Again, . . .

3. Rhetorical questions signaling an explanation of similarities or differences:

> What's the difference between these ideas?
> What sets these apart?

4. Stress emphasizing items being compared or their distinguishing characteristics:

> Now what about the women who *didn't* work outside of the home (as compared to those in the home)?
> Now the *employed* women (as compared to the women working at home) . . .

5. Body language suggesting a comparison:

> e.g., Hands can be used to emphasize different sides of a comparison/contrast.

on the one hand   on the other hand

Exercise

You will hear three lecture excerpts that include comparisons and contrasts. First, read the information about each excerpt. Then, while listening to the excerpts, take notes in the spaces provided.

Example

Excerpt from a lecture on evolution.

12–14 Million Yrs. Later — Fossils fr. Australopithecus (Aus.)
Similar to ♀ & ♂: walked upright
looked essentially like us
Differences: Aus. no cranium development
flat from nose up (like cat)
Aus. no chin

1. Excerpt from a lecture on ecology.

VOCABULARY
shrub: a bush, a woody plant

Typical deciduous woodland
Typical coniferous woodland

How might you rewrite these notes to emphasize the points of comparison?
Rewrite them below.

2. Excerpt from a lecture on human development.

VOCABULARY
innate: possessed at birth
predisposition: a tendency; an inclination

Empiricist View	Nativist View

3. Excerpt from an anthropology lecture on the development of societies.

VOCABULARY

hoe: a gardening tool with a flat blade and long handle used to break up soil

plow: a farming instrument, usually attached to an animal or vehicle, used to break up soil

agriculture: the science of farming

Diff. Betw. Horticulture (Digging Stick/Hoe Agriculture) & Plow Agriculture

How might you rewrite these notes to emphasize the points of comparison? Rewrite them below.

For additional practice recognizing and noting comparisons and contrasts (as a major or minor organizational pattern in a lecture), listen to any of the following lectures:

Lecture 10   The Near Surface of the Moon (page 124)
Lecture 11   Drink Your Green Tea! (page 132)
Lecture 13   Voter Turnout in the United States (page 140)
Lecture 17   Hall's Classification of Cultures (page 177)

⊞ Making a Generalization and Providing Evidence

In this case, the lecturer's goal is to make a generalization and provide evidence for that generalization. There are two varieties of this organizational plan, which differ in how the generalization is stated in relation to the evidence. In the first variety, the generalization *precedes* the evidence. In the second variety, the generalization *follows* the evidence.

Most often the generalization *precedes* the evidence. A model might look like the following:

> Generalization about intended topic
>
> +
>
> Evidence for the generalization
>
> +
>
> (Optional) Restatement of the generalization

In the following lecture notes, the generalization precedes the evidence:

Correlation Exists betw. Diet & Cancer

— immigrant cancer rates change to host country by 3rd generation

(even if both countries have similar pollution & food contamination rates)

e.g., Japanese immigrants to U.S. — ↓ stomach cancer &

↑ colon cancer than native Japanese

native Japanese diet — ↓ calories & ↓ fat

Notice that when the generalization and evidence are organized in this way, the listener's task is to be especially attentive at the beginning in order to understand the generalization that the lecturer is trying to make. Once the generalization is understood, the listener can relax a bit while listening and noting the evidence for the generalization.

At other times, the generalization *follows* the evidence. In this case, the lecturer leads the audience to a generalization. The generalization is presented at the end, in the form of a conclusion. A model might look like the following:

> Statement of intended topic
>
> +
>
> Evidence in form of anecdote(s), observation(s), test description(s), narrative(s) and/or factual detail(s) regarding topic
>
> +
>
> Generalization (conclusion) based on evidence

In the following lecture notes, the generalization follows the evidence:

Effect of Mother's Drinking Habits on Fetus:

   Experiment

      Procedure: — rat's pregnancy correlated w/ human pregnancy

               — at peak of brain development, rats given equivalent

                of human alcoholic alcohol intake

      Results: — offspring of "alcoholic" rats   — no diff. in body wt.

                                          — behavioral diff.

                                        — brain wt. 19% less

                                            than control group

∴ Pregnant ♀ should avoid excessive use of alcohol

Notice that when the generalization and evidence are organized in this way, the listener's task is to follow the speaker's train of thought and be especially attentive for the final conclusions.

EXAMPLES OF CUES TO RECOGNIZING A GENERALIZATION AND EVIDENCE

1. Words or phrases signaling a generalization or conclusion:

   Thus, . . .
   Therefore, . . .
   In conclusion, . . .
   To conclude, . . .

2. Phrases referring to previous evidence and signaling a conclusion:

   This shows (demonstrates, implies, proves, etc.) that . . .
   Taking all of this into account, we can see (conclude, assume, predict, etc.) that . . .
   Obviously (clearly, logically, etc.), X tells (shows, demonstrates to us, etc.) how . . .
   It should be apparent (obvious, clear, etc.), then, that . . .
   Based on X, we can assume (conclude, predict, etc.) that . . .
   What we have seen indicates that . . .

3. Phrases or sentences signaling evidence:

   This has been shown (proven, demonstrated, etc.) by . . .

4. Rhetorical questions signaling evidence:

   How do we know this?
   Is this true?
   What allows us to say this?

5. Rhetorical questions signaling a generalization:

> What can we conclude from this?
> What does this prove (demonstrate, show, etc.)?

Exercise

You will hear three lecture excerpts containing generalizations and evidence. First, read the information about each excerpt. Then, while listening to the excerpts, take notes in the spaces provided.

Example

Excerpt from a lecture on how working outside the home affects women.

evidence	Physical Benefits — ♀ Employed or Not?
	in past ♂ > heart-attack rate than ♀
	Why? ♂ employed? ♀ not?
	now 50% ♀ in job market but still ≠ heart-attack rate
generalization	∴ No physical benefit or risk ~ =

1. Excerpt from a lecture on memory-improving drugs.

VOCABULARY
maze: an enclosed system with many confusing pathways

generalization	
evidence	

2. Excerpt from a lecture on language learning.

evidence	
generalization	∴

3. Excerpt from a lecture on Asian-Pacific immigration to the United States.

   VOCABULARY
   heterogeneous: consisting of different kinds
   dialect: a regional variety of a language

generalization

evidence

For additional practice recognizing and noting generalizations and evidence (as a major or minor organizational pattern in a lecture), listen to any of the following lectures:

Lecture 3   American Attitudes toward Work (page 34)
Lecture 12   Drink Your Green Tea! (page 132)
Lecture 16   Earthquakes: Can They Be Predicted? (page 168)

⊞ Tangents

When people write, they have time to edit their words and eliminate information that does not fit. When people speak, this is impossible once words are spoken. Speakers more frequently and more easily go off on tangents; that is, they digress from the main point. This may be an intentional tangent, such as an interesting story, a joke, or an important piece of information that suddenly comes to mind. It may also be unintentional, such as when speakers go from one point to another and eventually find themselves far from the intended topic.

As a listener, you need to recognize tangents so that they don't confuse you and distract you from the key points of the lecture. They also might provide a lighthearted break from continuous note-taking.

Although tangents are sometimes preceded by specific cues, more often they are not. However, cues are often used after a tangent to bring the audience back to the original subject.

EXAMPLES OF CUES TO RECOGNIZING TANGENTS

1. Phrases or sentences signaling a possible tangent:

   Now before I go on, . . .
   By the way, . . .
   Let me talk about X for a minute.
   Let me make a parenthesis.
   That reminds me of a story.

2. Words or phrases following a tangent:

> Now, . . .
> Anyway, . . .
> Okay.
> Back to what we were talking about, . . .

3. Rhetorical questions following a tangent and signaling a return to the original subject:

> What were we talking about?
> Where were we?

Exercise

 You will hear four lecture excerpts that include tangential information. First, read the questions about each excerpt. Then listen to the excerpt without taking notes. After listening, answer the question.

1. Excerpt from a lecture on the theory of the aquatic evolution of humans.

In the main part of the lecture, the speaker talks about his view that humans have descended from aquatic animals as well as land-based animals. What is the tangential information?

_____

2. Excerpt from an ecology lecture on the moderating effect of water on the climate.

In the main part of the lecture, the speaker talks about the two reasons why water has a moderating effect on climate: (1) its specific heat and (2) the two forms of latent heat. What is the tangential information?

_____

3. Excerpt from a lecture on the spread of disease. (Note the use of the cue "but anyway" when the author finishes the tangent and wants to signal a return to the main subject.)

In the main part of the lecture, the speaker talks about how the bubonic plague typically spreads. What is the tangential information?

_____

4. Excerpt from a lecture on family systems.

> VOCABULARY
> **kin**: relatives
> **vestige**: evidence of something that no longer exists

In the main part of the lecture, the speaker describes the three types of marriage payments: bride price, dowry, and bride service. What is the tangential information?

_____

LECTURE COMPREHENSION AND NOTE-TAKING PRACTICE

◑ Goals

- Practice listening for the larger picture in lectures of five to twenty minutes
- Practice recognizing the organizational plans used in lectures of five to twenty minutes
- Practice taking notes on lectures emphasizing different organizational plans
- Practice using notes to answer various test-type questions
- Learn and use vocabulary from lectures and related readings in exercises, discussions, presentations, and other follow-up activities

LECTURE

6 HOW TO DEAL WITH STRESS

PRE-LECTURE READING AND DISCUSSION

The scale on pages 84–85 was developed by Dr. Thomas Holmes and Dr. Richard Rahe in their research on how stress affects health.

Try the scale for yourself. Give yourself the indicated points for each life event that you have experienced in the past year. Then discuss your answers to the questions that follow.

stress
tension
anxiety
irritability

tense
anxious
irritable

to cope

stressors
sources of stress

insomnia
shortness/tightness of
breath
accelerated breathing
muscle spasm
nervous tic
high blood pressure

Additional
Vocabulary

The Social Readjustment Rating Scale

Life Event   *Mean Value*

1. Death of spouse 100
2. Divorce 73
3. Marital separation from mate 65
4. Detention in jail or other institution 63
5. Death of a close family member 63
6. Major personal injury or illness 53
7. Marriage 50
8. Being fired at work 47
9. Marital reconciliation with mate 45
10. Retirement from work 45
11. Major change in the health or behavior of a family member 44
12. Pregnancy 40
13. Sexual difficulties 39
14. Gaining a new family member (e.g., through birth, adoption,
    elder moving in) 39
15. Major business readjustment (e.g., merger, reorganization,
    bankruptcy) 39
16. Major change in financial state (i.e., much worse or better off
    than usual) 38
17. Death of a close friend 37
18. Changing to a different line of work 36
19. Major change in the number of arguments with spouse
    (i.e., much more or less than usual) 35
20. Taking out a mortgage or loan for a major purchase
    (e.g., for a home or business) 31
21. Foreclosure on a mortgage or loan 30
22. Major change in responsibilities at work (e.g., promotion,
    demotion, or lateral transfer) 29
23. Son or daughter leaving home (e.g., for marriage or college) 29
24. Trouble with in-laws 29
25. Outstanding personal achievement 28
26. Spouse beginning or ceasing work outside the home 26
27. Beginning or ceasing formal schooling 26
28. Major change in living conditions (e.g., building a new home,
    remodeling, or deterioration of home or neighborhood) 25
29. Revision of personal habits (e.g., dress, manners, or associations) . . 24
30. Trouble with the boss 23
31. Major change in working hours or conditions 20
32. Change in residence 20
33. Changing to a new school 20
34. Major change in usual type and/or amount of recreation 19
35. Major change in church activities (i.e., attending much more or
    less than usual) 19

36. Major change in social activities (e.g., clubs, movies, or visiting)	18
37. Taking out a mortgage or loan for a lesser purchase (e.g., for a car, TV, or freezer)	17
38. Major change in sleeping habits (e.g., much more or less sleep, or change in part of day when asleep)	16
39. Major change in number of family get-togethers (e.g., much more or less than usual)	15
40. Major change in eating habits (e.g., much more or less food intake, or very different meal hours or surroundings)	15
41. Vacation	13
42. Christmas	12
43. Minor violations of the law (e.g., traffic tickets, jaywalking, or disturbing the peace)	11

1. What is your "stress score"? _____ How does your score compare with your classmates' scores?

2. According to this scale, is stress always bad?

3. Would this scale be appropriate for all ages? If not, how might it differ for adolescents? older teens? Would this scale be appropriate for all cultures? If not, why not?

4. In their study, Dr. Holmes and Dr. Rahe found that 79 percent of those who scored more than 300 points on this scale developed a major illness within the year that followed. Do you think this proves that stress causes illness? Why or why not?

5. Do you think that your stress score is too high? What steps can people take to reduce the effects of stress on the body?

PREPARING FOR THE LECTURE

The title of the lecture is "How to Deal with Stress." What do you expect the lecturer to talk about? Brainstorm ideas with your classmates.

LISTENING FOR THE LARGER PICTURE

 Read the following summaries before the lecture begins. Then, listen to the lecture once without taking notes. After listening, circle the letter of the summary that most closely describes the lecture.

    a. The lecturer primarily compares the two types of stress: negative stress and positive stress. Then, the lecturer lists ways to deal with negative stress.

    b. The lecturer primarily talks about the health hazards associated with stress and lists the reasons why people should avoid stress.

    c. The lecturer defines stress and talks about two types of stress. Then, the lecturer focuses on the main part of the talk, which involves a list of ways that one can deal with stress appropriately.

    d. The lecturer states that stress is hazardous in itself and then provides evidence for that generalization. Finally, the lecturer lists ways to eliminate stress from one's life.

ORGANIZATION

The lecture primarily demonstrates two organizational plans: *defining a term* and *listing subtopics*. The lecturer begins by defining stress, giving a simple definition, and then expanding that definition with additional details. The lecturer then lists five ways to deal with stress appropriately, giving examples or additional details about each way as needed.

DEFINING VOCABULARY

 The following words and expressions were used in the lecture that you just heard. You may remember the contexts in which you heard them. You will hear an additional example of each word or expression in a new context. After listening, circle the letter of the definition that most closely matches what you think the word or expression means.

1. virtually
   a. rarely; almost never the case
   b. more or less true in practical terms
   c. ideally; as it would be in the ideal world

2. immune
   a. unaffected; invulnerable
   b. affected; vulnerable
   c. sickly; ill

3. to adapt
   a. to take for one's own
   b. to raise another person's child
   c. to adjust for a particular use

4. incentive
   a. a stressful position
   b. something that motivates a person to act
   c. a person who does not have feelings for others

5. hazardous
   a. unpleasant
   b. unusual
   c. dangerous

6. to monitor
   a. to protect
   b. to check regularly
   c. to harm or damage

7. regardless of
   a. in spite of; without concern about
   b. because of; due to
   c. next to; adjacent to

8. out of one's hands
   a. not in one's interest
   b. not in one's field of vision
   c. not in one's power

9. inevitable
   a. unable to be considered
   b. unable to be enjoyed
   c. unable to be avoided or prevented

10. to pace
    a. to adjust the speed or timing
    b. to run a long-distance competition
    c. to receive a prize

NOTE-TAKING PRACTICE

 Listen to the lecture a second time. Take notes using the following format. The comments in the left margin serve to remind you of the organization of the lecture.

introduction	
definition of stress	What is stress?
types of stress and examples	
ways to cope with stress	Ways to deal w/stress appropriately:
	1.
	2.
	3.
	4.
	5.
conclusion	

Review and revise your notes. Add information that you remember. If helpful, consider rewriting your notes. Make the relationship between ideas clear and make important ideas stand out.

POST-LECTURE DISCUSSION

Discuss your answers to the following questions in small groups.

1. The lecturer's first suggestion for dealing with stress appropriately is to recognize your own stress signals. The lecturer mentions that people have different early signs of stress. What are *your* early stress signals?

2. What do you think the following quote means?

> *I remember the story of the old man who said on his deathbed that he had had a lot of trouble in his life, most of which never happened.*
> — **Winston Churchill, *British Prime Minister* (1874–1965)**

How does this idea relate to your own life?

3. Talk about a stressful time in your life. What did you do (and/or what could you have done) to manage the stress better?

USING YOUR NOTES

Use your notes to answer the following questions.

1. According to this lecture, stress is the body's
   a. nonspecific response to any unpleasant demand placed on it.
   b. specific response to any unpleasant demand placed on it.
   c. nonspecific response to any demand placed on it, pleasant or unpleasant.
   d. specific response to any demand placed on it, pleasant or unpleasant.

2. In what field of study did the term *stress* originate? _____

3. What is *eustress*? _____
_____

4. The lecturer lists five ways to deal with stress appropriately. What are they?
   a. _____
   b. _____
   c. _____
   d. _____
   e. _____

5. True or False? _____ Stress, in itself, is hazardous.

COMPARING IDEAS

1. In small groups, compare notes. What information do you have that your classmates don't? What information do they have that you don't?

2. In small groups, compare your answers to the preceding questions. If you have different answers, check your notes and discuss your reasons for making your choices.

3. Compare your rewritten notes to the sample rewritten notes in Appendix C. Notice the organization. Is yours similar or different? Are your notes equally effective in making important ideas stand out?

USING VOCABULARY

 You will hear vocabulary from the lecture in different contexts. Listen before reading each exercise. After listening, circle the letter of the sentence that most closely paraphrases the information that you heard.

Group A

1. a. He slept poorly last night.
   b. He slept well last night.

2. a. He is easily annoyed because he doesn't sleep well.
   b. He doesn't sleep well because he is easily annoyed by things that happen to him.
   c. He is in a wonderful mood because of his good night's sleep.

3. a. His wife is affected by the noise outside the window.
   b. His wife is not affected by the noise outside the window.

4. a. Traffic speeds by at certain hours of the night.
   b. Traffic rarely speeds by at night.
   c. Traffic speeds by at all hours of the night.

5. a. The husband is giving up on solving the noise problem or complaining to the authorities.
   b. The husband is gathering evidence before he complains to the authorities.
   c. The husband is changing his behavior so he can get used to the situation instead of complaining.

Group B

1. a. People who have been burned tend to have difficulties handling the stress in all or part of their lives.
   b. People who experience burnout have a hard time dealing with all or part of their lives.

2. a. According to psychologists, people who don't know how to manage their time and energy will probably experience burnout.
   b. According to psychologists, people who get burned should probably not move around too quickly and should adjust the number of activities they plan in each day.

RETAINING VOCABULARY

Write ten words from the lecture, reading, and discussion that you would like to remember. Use each word in an example that will remind you of its meaning.

Example

insomnia: I look tired this morning because I had insomnia last night and only had two hours of sleep.

1. _____

_____

2. _____

_____

3. _____

_____

4. _____

_____

5. _____

_____

6. _____

_____

7. _____

_____

8. _____

_____

9. _____

_____

10. _____

_____

WRITING ACTIVITY

Write about a stressful event or time in your life and what you did to manage the stress then. Discuss whether the lecturer's suggestions for coping with stress were relevant in your situation. Could the lecturer's suggestions or any other techniques have helped you handle the stress better or differently?

PRE-LECTURE READING AND DISCUSSION

Vocabulary Related to Pollution

hazardous/toxic substance

haze
smog

fume
emission
waste (product)
pollutant

to contaminate
to corrode

to discharge
to dispose

natural resource

environment
ecology

Additional Vocabulary

Read the following excerpt from a magazine article about acid rain. When you have finished, discuss your answers to the questions that follow in small groups.

The International Acid Test

Anne LaBastille, *Sierra Magazine*

My log cabin looks out over a lake that has grown increasingly clear in recent years, with a strange layer of algae spreading across the bottom. Native trout are now scarce, as are certain types of fish-eating birds. Bullfrogs are few and far between. As much as a third of the virgin red spruce around the lake have died.

When I dropped a pH meter in the lake right after the snowmelt in 1985, it measured a very acidic 3.9. In the summer of 1979, it had measured 4.3, and in 1933, according to state records, it was a healthy 6.3.

I've noticed these and many other changes in the 20 years I've lived in the Adirondack Mountains of upstate New York, one of the regions hardest hit by acid rain. Many of my neighbors have had to replace their copper and lead plumbing with plastic lines as acidic waters corroded the pipes. At least 600 lakes and ponds in the Western Adirondacks have been acidified to some degree, and the red spruce forests on the higher peaks show extensive damage.

After studying the problems with acid rain in this country, I traveled to Scandinavia and Switzerland to take a look at the big picture. This foreign exposure revealed that acid fallout is not just an American or Canadian problem; it affects Europe and all densely populated, industrialized nations that use fossil fuels to produce energy.

Acid rain is also threatening trout high in the Rocky Mountains and sugar maples in Vermont and Ontario. It is dissolving India's Taj Mahal and is making some European game animals' organs unfit to eat. According to Earthscan, an independent news service, more than 16 million acres of forest in nine European countries have been damaged by acid rain. The Acropolis, the Tower of London, and Cologne Cathedral are also becoming victims. As one Danish architect commented, "These buildings are melting away like sugar candy." Even urban areas of Latin America and Africa are showing signs of damage.

1. LaBastille lists a number of effects of acid rain on the area around her home in the Adirondack Mountains, as well as effects of acid rain worldwide. What are those effects?

2. Had you heard of acid rain before reading this article? What do you know about it? Share your knowledge with your group.

PREPARING FOR THE LECTURE

The title of the lecture is "Acid Rain." What do you expect the lecturer to talk about? Brainstorm ideas with your classmates.

LISTENING FOR THE LARGER PICTURE

 Read the following questions before the lecture begins. Then, listen to the lecture once without taking notes. After listening, answer the questions.

The lecturer's goal is to tell the audience about _____ .

In order to do this, which of the following does the lecturer do? (Check all correct answers.)

_____ a. classifies the types of acid rain

_____ b. defines acid rain

_____ c. gives the causes of acid rain

_____ d. gives the effects of acid rain

_____ e. presents solutions to the problem of acid rain

_____ f. compares and contrasts acid rain to other forms of pollution

ORGANIZATION

Listen to the introduction one more time. The lecturer begins the talk by stating a number of surprising facts and statistics about acid rain. Why would a lecturer choose to begin in this way?

The lecture primarily demonstrates two organizational plans: *giving a definition* and *describing a causal relationship*. At the beginning, there is a simple definition of acid rain. The lecturer then goes into detail about that definition by, for example, comparing the pH of acid rain to that of "pure" rain. The lecturer later gives a number of sources (or causes) of acid rain and then gives a number of its effects. The lecturer ends by very briefly stating some possible solutions.

DEFINING VOCABULARY

The following words and expressions were used in the lecture that you just heard. You may remember the contexts in which you heard them. You will hear an additional example of each word or expression in a new context. After listening, circle the letter of the definition that most closely matches what you think the word or expression means.

1. corrosion
   a. the process of building with metal
   b. the process of deteriorating or wearing down (especially by chemical action)
   c. the process of melting (especially by applying heat)

2. ecosystem
   a. the system that connects animals to each other
   b. the system that connects plants and animals to their physical environment
   c. the system that connects the economy and the environment

3. precipitation
   a. water in any form (e.g., rain, snow, sleet) that falls on the earth
   b. dry weather (e.g., the climate of the desert)
   c. hot weather (e.g., the climate of regions located near the equator)

4. source
   a. a place from which something originates
   b. money
   c. a flavorful liquid served over food

5. emission
   a. something released and sent out (e.g., radiation, gas)
   b. an automobile part
   c. a poor driving habit

6. vulnerable
   a. easily attacked or harmed
   b. ready to attack
   c. prepared for an attack

7. to level off
   a. to rise; to go up
   b. to decline; to go down
   c. to become steady after rising or declining

8. adverse
   a. negative
   b. positive
   c. expected

9. to attribute
   a. to smoke a lot
   b. to die suddenly
   c. to regard as the cause

10. toxic
    a. expensive
    b. tasty
    c. poisonous

11. glacier
    a. a huge accident at sea
    b. a huge mass of moving ice
    c. a huge ship

12. alternative energy
    a. energy that comes from a nontypical source (e.g., wind power)
    b. energy that is caused by the decomposition of organic material (e.g., oil, gas, or coal)
    c. energy that is used in large quantities

13. airborne
    a. carried by or through the air
    b. giving birth in the air
    c. a fear or terror of flying

NOTE-TAKING PRACTICE

 Listen to the lecture a second time. Take notes using the following format. The comments in the left margin serve to remind you of the organization of the lecture.

introduction

definition of acid rain

Acid rain

details about
definition

cause & effect
explanation

Causes

    Nitrogen sources

    Sulfur sources

Effects

    On aquatic ecosystems

    On forests

    On architectural structures

    On health

conclusion

_____

Review and revise your notes. Add information that you remember. If helpful, consider rewriting your notes. Make the relationship between ideas clear and make important ideas stand out.

POST-LECTURE DISCUSSION

Discuss your answers to the following questions in small groups.

1. Due to increased use of fossil fuels (i.e., coal, oil, and gas) and increased industrialization, our world has become increasingly polluted. Acid rain is only one type of pollution. Do you think our industrial gains and improved standard of living outweigh the costs to our health and the environment? Or do you believe that the costs, in terms of environmental damage, outweigh the benefits of our more industrialized lifestyle? Justify your answer.
2. Does your lifestyle contribute to the problem of acid rain? If so, how?
3. How can consumers reduce the amount of sulfur and nitrogen emissions? How likely are you to make these changes in your lifestyle?

USING YOUR NOTES

Use your notes to answer the following questions.

1. When nitrogen is released into the atmosphere, it combines with oxygen and hydrogen to become _____ .

2. Where does the nitrogen in acid rain come from? In what percentages?

   _____

   _____

3. Where does the sulfur in acid rain come from? In what percentages?

   _____

   _____

4. True or False?

_____ a. Acid rain refers only to *rain* that contains a high level of acid.

_____ b. Acid rain is particularly the United States's problem.

_____ c. Theoretically, pure rain has a pH of 1.4.

_____ d. Lakes affected by acid rain always look unhealthy.

_____ e. Trees are affected by acid rain because it destroys their roots.

_____ f. Scientists have found a direct cause/effect relationship between acid rain and human illness.

_____ g. Acid rain has always occurred at the current levels. It is only at the current time that we have become aware of its dangers.

COMPARING IDEAS

1. In small groups, compare notes. What information do you have that your classmates don't? What information do they have that you don't?

2. In small groups, compare your answers to the preceding questions. If you have different answers, check your notes and discuss your reasons for making your choices.

3. Compare your rewritten notes to the sample rewritten notes in Appendix C. Notice the organization. Is yours similar or different? Are your notes equally effective in making important ideas stand out?

USING VOCABULARY

You will hear a short talk about the effects of acid rain on the lakes of southern Norway. After listening, read the following summary and fill in the blanks with words from the vocabulary list below. (You may change the verb forms and tenses.)

airborne	adverse effects	source	to attribute
precipitation	ecosystem	vulnerable	toxic

The talk is about the effect of acid rain on lakes in southern Norway.

The fish, in particular, seemed to be (1) _____

to the acid rain. For example, in a 33,000 sq. km. area, there were definite

(2) _____ on the fish population. In a 13,000 sq. km.

area, all the fish died. Scientists (3) _____ the death

of the fish to two factors: the direct effect of the acid, and the fact that the acid rain

causes aluminum from the surrounding soil to enter the lake, killing the fish because

aluminum is (4) _____ to fish. The death of these fish

has had an effect on the (5) _____ of the area because

animals are losing an important (6) _____ of food.

RETAINING VOCABULARY

Write ten words from the lecture, reading, and discussion that you would like to remember. Use each word in an example that will remind you of its meaning.

Example

emission: One way to control air pollution is to require that emissions from cars be measured and reduced if necessary.

1. _____

_____

2. _____

_____

3. _____

_____

4. _____

_____

5. _____

_____

6. _____

_____

7. _____

_____

8. _____

_____

9. _____

_____

10. _____

_____

SPEAKING AND LISTENING ACTIVITY

Read an article from the library or the Internet about a current environmental issue (e.g., acid rain, air pollution, water pollution, the destruction of the rain forest). Prepare a five-minute presentation. Explain the main ideas of the article and conclude with your opinion and/or evaluation of these ideas.

PRE-LECTURE READING AND DISCUSSION

Vocabulary
Related to
Archaeology

excavation
dig
site

remains
remnant
ruins

to excavate

to inhabit/inhabitant
to reside/resident
to dwell/dweller

shelter
residence
dwelling

tribe
clan

legend
myth

archaeologist

Additional
Vocabulary

The following is a composite made up of details discovered at several archaeological digs. There are no written records of these events, no pictures or legends passed down through the years. Read this excerpt from a scientific magazine describing life more than three thousand years ago.

The site was first inhabited in 1250 B.C. by a small tribe of forty or fifty men, women, and children. The women wore bright beaded jewelry, and many of the men had their front teeth sanded down, perhaps as a symbol of bravery.

They came from somewhere farther north, searching for food and shelter. On their arrival, they felled several dozen trees near the creek, choosing only the hardest woods to carve into tent poles. There was an accident and one young brave died of ax wounds.

That spring over 3,000 years ago, the men went out on a hunt, bringing down at least seventy young bison—enough to keep the tribe well fed and clothed. The carcasses were hauled to a cave in the nearby mountainside for butchering. Most of the meat was later roasted over open fire pits in the valley below, while the tougher parts were stone-boiled for soup. For this kind of cooking, stones were heated in a fire until red hot. Then the stones were placed in a pot of water to make the water boil.

The bones of the bison were kept in the cave. Some were whittled into spear shafts and other tools, but only two of the best tribal craftsmen were allowed to handle this job. The unusable bones were dumped into a garbage heap toward the back of the cave. Here, broken spearheads, shattered pottery, and even human excrement were discarded.

While the men hunted, the women gathered nuts and berries. Hackberries were the favorite. That first year was a prosperous one. Over twenty-three inches of rain fell. The area was lush and provided sustenance for over a hundred species of animals and dozens of varieties of plants. The tribe could keep a few wild dogs as pets.

A wandering tradesman came to visit that year and brought seeds for a new kind of edible plant—seeds that the women used to start a crop. The visitor also brought trinkets: turquoise beads and strange bits of a sharp-edged material called obsidian, which had been found near a faraway volcano. Together with bits of shell and animal teeth, these were brought to the women's work tent to make more necklaces.

In the year 1245 B.C., a great drought hit the area, followed by a hard winter. Crops shriveled. The creek dried out. Many of the tribespeople, including an eight-month-old baby and a seventy-year-old tribal elder, died from hunger or cold. The tribe resorted to cannibalism, eating the remains of their dead to keep alive.

The area began to change. The forests and lush fields were replaced by a parched and dusty landscape. The tribe was forced to move on in search of better hunting grounds.

While you were reading, were you surprised at how much archaeologists were able to learn about life so long ago? Do you know how they were able to reach these conclusions?

Work in small groups to suggest what evidence might have led the archaeologists to each of these conclusions. Use your imagination and your knowledge. The first one has been done as an example.

When you have finished, compare your ideas with those of the other groups. Which seem like the best answers?

Conclusion	Possible Evidence
1. The site was inhabited by forty to fifty men, women, and children.	They found skeletons.
2. The women wore bright beaded jewelry.	
3. The men had their front teeth sanded down, perhaps as a symbol of bravery.	
4. They came from somewhere farther north searching for food and shelter.	
5. On their arrival, they felled several dozen trees near the creek, choosing only the hardest woods to carve into tent poles.	
6. There was an accident and one young brave died of ax wounds.	
7. That spring, the men went out on a hunt, bringing down at least seventy young bison.	
8. The carcasses were hauled to a cave in the nearby mountainside for butchering.	
9. Most of the meat was roasted over open fire pits in the valley below while the tougher parts were stone-boiled for soup.	
10. Only two of the best tribal craftsmen were allowed to handle the job of whittling bones into spear shafts and other tools.	
11. That first year over twenty-three inches of rain fell.	
12. A wandering tradesman came to visit that year and brought seeds for a new kind of edible plant—seeds that the women used to start a crop.	
13. In the year 1245 B.C., a great drought hit the area, followed by a hard winter.	
14. The tribe was forced to move on in search of better hunting grounds.	

PREPARING FOR THE LECTURE

The title of the lecture is "Archaeological Dating Methods." What do you expect the lecturer to talk about? Brainstorm ideas with your classmates.

LISTENING FOR THE LARGER PICTURE

Read the following questions before the lecture begins. Then, listen to the lecture once without taking notes. After listening, fill in the blanks and answer the questions.

1. The lecturer talks about two kinds of archaeological dating methods:

   _____ and _____ .

   In particular, the lecturer talks about the latter method's drawbacks and

   recent _____ .

2. What do you remember about the first kind of archaeological dating method?

   _____

   _____

   _____

3. What do you remember about the second kind of archaeological dating method?

   _____

   _____

   _____

ORGANIZATION

The overall organizational plan of this lecture is *exemplification*. The topic is archaeological dating methods, and two examples of these dating methods are discussed in detail. In addition, the lecture includes an explanation of a *process*, the process of C-14 dating.

DEFINING VOCABULARY

The following words and expressions were used in the lecture that you just heard. You may remember the contexts in which you heard them. You will hear an additional example of each word or expression in a new context. After listening, use context clues to write a definition for each word or expression.

1. climatic _____

2. cross section _____

3. drought _____

4. cold spell _____

5. abundant _____

6. unstable _____

7. to disintegrate _____

8. to diminish _____

9. to tally _____

10. to emit _____

11. drawback _____

12. to cross-check _____

NOTE-TAKING PRACTICE

Listen to the lecture a second time. Take notes using the following format. The comments in the left margin serve to remind you of the organization of the lecture.

introduction	
	Archaeological Dating Methods
example 1: dendrochronology	Dendrochronology
details	
example 2: C-14 dating	Carbon-14 Dating Method
process	
advances	Recent advances in C-14 dating: Accelerated Mass Spectrometry (AMS)

limitations	C-14 dating is limited to		years	
conclusions				

Review and revise your notes. Add information that you remember. If helpful, consider rewriting your notes. Make the relationship between ideas clear and make important ideas stand out.

POST-LECTURE READING AND DISCUSSION

Would you be interested in working with researchers who are investigating the prehistoric past? Earthwatch Institute International is an international nonprofit organization that supports scientific field research through programs that put volunteers and scientists together at a research site. Though projects often take years, volunteers join the team for one to three weeks. Read through the following project descriptions to answer these questions about each one:

- What are the researchers trying to find out?
- What will volunteers be doing?
- What are the working and living conditions? (Consider site, climate, recreation opportunities, etc.)

After reading the descriptions, decide which program would best fit your interests and preferences. In small groups, explain your choice and at least three of your reasons.

Project 1: Dinosaur Footprints

Yorkshire, England. Just as a good tracker today can tell you what animal made a track, its age, sex, size, speed of travel, and something about its behavior ("It's headed north toward the river"), a good detective can read similar information from the footprints of extinct creatures, such as dinosaurs. If you're lacking physical remains—as is often true of the middle Jurassic dinosaurs of 165 million 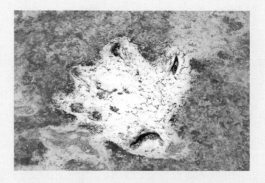 years ago, when many groups of dinosaurs were developing—then the tracks they left become even more critical. One track Dr. Martin Whyte and Dr. Mike Romano [of the University of Sheffield, England] have found, for instance, was from a sauropod dinosaur, which they estimated to be about six feet at the hip joint and up to 35 feet long. He was plodding along at half a mile an hour in a rich marshy area. Was he eating? Did he have companions? Was he full-grown? Was he a she?

Paleontologists have long known that the spectacular seacoast and upland moors of Yorkshire harbored lots of dinosaur tracks, but you have the chance to be among the first to locate and systematically study them and help preserve them. You'll search along the shore and valleys for footprints. The data teams collect will help determine the number and proportions of species over time that made Yorkshire home, and the size, behavior, and speed of the footprint-makers. Your findings will thus help piece together what kinds of dinosaurs once roamed Yorkshire, how they lived and evolved, and what their world was like.

RESEARCH AREA

The Heritage Coastline is a national park encompassing cliffs and sandy bays. Nearby towns are littered with Roman, Viking, and medieval ruins. Expect typically British weather: changeable from blue skies to fog to rain, and daytime temperatures around 60° F.

VOLUNTEER TASKS

Working in small crews, volunteers will walk transects, searching the coastline and valleys for dinosaur footprints. Teams will map, photograph, and trace prints directly onto overlays, help make casts of selected tracks, and record geological features. Skills in photography, drawing, mapping, and geological survey will come in handy. Be prepared to scramble among large, slippery boulders on the shore and to climb steep valley sides among boulders and scrub.

Project 2: Search for Neanderthals

Sima de las Palomas and Cueva Negra, Murcia, Spain. Two years ago, Dr. Michael Walker [of Murcia University, Spain] began excavating Cueva Negra ("Black Cave") in the mountains of southeastern Spain. His efforts have been rewarded with discoveries of teeth from Neanderthal humans, remnants of extinct animals, and the stone tools used to butcher those animals.

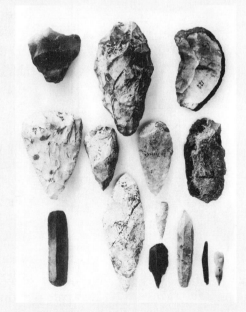

The second site, named Cabezo Gordo ("Big Hill"), was discovered accidentally in 1991 when a young explorer, investigating an old mine, inadvertently dislodged a bone with human teeth attached. The remains were indeed those of Neanderthal Man. Subsequent excavations of this site have yielded the remains of twenty Neanderthals, together with their tools and the bones of extinct animals, including lions and panthers, that had also inhabited this site.

Paleoanthropologists want to learn more about Neanderthals, who disappeared from the archaeological record about 35,000 years ago. Were the Neanderthals the true ancestors of modern humans in Europe? Was Europe populated by travelers from the Near East or Africa after the Neanderthals died out? Perhaps some of the information we discover in Murcia will help answer those questions.

RESEARCH AREA

Both research sites are located in the province of Murcia in southeastern Spain. Murcia is extremely dry during the summer months with a very warm coastal region (85° F to 105° F). The hills and mountains, rocky slopes and cliffs, are blanketed by the fragrant cover of thyme, juniper, laurel, and rosemary. In contrast, the valleys are lush and green. Murcia, an important Muslim kingdom until the thirteenth century, was once known for its silk industry. Mulberry orchards have since been replaced by peaches, tomatoes, lemons, oranges, almonds, and olives.

VOLUNTEER TASKS

Earthwatch team members will be assigned to task groups and by rotation will have the opportunity to work in all aspects of the project. Morning assignments will involve excavation and removing excavated material for sieving. Afternoon assignments will include washing and drying excavated materials from the morning's work and preliminary classification of the dry materials from the previous day. This project is not suitable for those with cardiovascular ailments.

USING YOUR NOTES

Use your notes to answer the following questions.

1. True or False?
   _____ a. In order to do a dendrochronological analysis, scientists must count all the tree rings.
   _____ b. By doing a dendrochronological analysis, scientists can tell when a drought or a cold spell occurred.
   _____ c. Dendrochronological analyses are limited to only about 100 years.
   _____ d. The carbon-14 dating method is based on the idea that all living organisms contain C-14, a radioactive isotope.
   _____ e. The carbon-14 dating method is based on the idea that an organism's carbon-14 level changes while it is alive.
   _____ f. One drawback of the C-14 dating method is that the radioactivity is dangerous to the researcher.
   _____ g. Accelerator Mass Spectrometry measures the C-14 atoms, not the radioactive emissions.
   _____ h. Carbon-14 dating does not work well with objects older than 16,000 years.
   _____ i. Most of the time, scientists use at least two dating methods in order to ensure accuracy.

2. A pale tree ring indicates _____ .
   a. winter   c. a drought   e. abundant water
   b. spring   d. a cold spell   and sunlight

3. A thick tree ring indicates _____ .
   a. winter   c. a drought   e. abundant water
   b. spring   d. a cold spell   and sunlight

4. What is the half-life of C-14? _____

5. How is Accelerated Mass Spectrometer dating an improvement over older C-14 dating methods?

_____

_____

6. Describe how an archaeologist would do a dendrochronological analysis.

_____

_____

_____

_____

COMPARING IDEAS

1. In small groups, compare notes. What information do you have that your classmates don't? What information do they have that you don't?
2. In small groups, compare your answers to the preceding questions. If you have different answers, check your notes and discuss your reasons for making your choices.
3. Compare your rewritten notes to the sample rewritten notes in Appendix C. Notice the organization. Is yours similar or different? Are your notes equally effective in making important ideas stand out?

USING VOCABULARY

Listen to each item. Then, paraphrase what you hear by filling in the blanks with words from the vocabulary list. (You may change the verb forms and tenses.)

legends	_to deteriorate_	_drought_	_site_
drawback	_to diminish_	_inhabitants_	_to emit_
cold spell	_to excavate_	_abundant_	

1. According to _____ , a very powerful tribe of people

   lived at this _____ . Archaeologists

   _____ the area in order to find out the truth.

2. An analysis of a cross-section of the tree indicates a _____

   during the year 2000 B.C. that _____ the food supply.

3. The primary _____ of the older C-14 dating method is

   that it requires a fairly large sample.

4. In 1450, there was a period of _____ rainfall, and this

   caused the _____ to move to higher ground.

RETAINING VOCABULARY

Write ten words from the lecture, reading, and discussion that you would like to remember. Use each word in an example that will remind you of its meaning.

Example

drought: The drought lasted for one month, and during that time not a single drop of water fell.

1. _____

_____

2. _____

_____

3. _____

_____

4. _____

_____

5. _____

_____

6. _____

_____

7. _____

_____

8. _____

_____

9. _____

_____

10. _____

_____

WRITING ACTIVITY

Write a letter to the director of Earthwatch Institute International, expressing your interest in volunteering for one of the projects on pages 102–104. In your letter, explain why the project interests you and what skills you have that might be useful for the project. Add questions that you might have about the project, the research area, the living conditions, and the volunteer activities.

PRE-LECTURE DISCUSSION

Discuss the following in small groups.

1. Each of the following drawings attempts to communicate ideas and feelings. Discuss what you believe the artists were attempting to communicate. As a group, decide which drawing you think communicates its ideas most effectively.

   a. Drawing given to Amnesty International by Pablo Picasso

   b. The Amnesty International Logo

   c. Graphic from an Amnesty International Publication

Vocabulary Related to Human Rights

freedom of
   speech
   press
   movement
   assembly
   association
   religion

human rights
   violation/abuse

civil liberties

torture
execution

to deprive of freedom
to hold in custody
to detain
detention

censorship

to dissent
dissenter

to persecute
persecution

amnesty

Additional Vocabulary

2. Judging from the discussion and the graphics, can you guess what Amnesty International does? Had you heard of Amnesty International before today? If so, what had you heard? What does "human rights" mean to you?

PREPARING FOR THE LECTURE

 Listen to the introduction of the lecture. The introduction will tell you what Amnesty International does. Fill in the blanks with the missing dates, statistics, and other information.

Amnesty International
Founded in
One of largest & most active human rights organizations
In   —   members & supporters in   countries
In   — received the
In   — given award by UN for outstanding achievement in human rights
Concerned strictly with
Seeks release of "prisoners of conscience" who are
Works for fair trials within reasonable time periods for <u>all</u> political prisoners
Acts for protection of all persons against torture
Works for abolition of death penalty

The introduction ends with the following words:

> . . . OK . . . what I'm specifically going to focus on in this lecture . . . now that I've told you a little bit about the organization . . . are some of the specific principles that underlie some of Amnesty International's activities . . . and probably contribute to its success . . . OK . . . and there are eight principles in particular that I'm going to talk about . . .

What do you expect the lecturer to talk about in the remainder of the lecture?

LISTENING FOR THE LARGER PICTURE

 Listen to the complete lecture. While listening, note the eight principles underlying Amnesty International's activities and success. You will hear several details describing each one of these principles. At this time, only note the principles.

Eight Principles Underlying Amnesty International's Activities and Success

1. _____

2. _____

3. _____

4. _____

5. _____

6. _____

7. _____

8. _____

Compare your list of principles to a classmate's list. Discuss whether you have similar ideas about what each principle means.

ORGANIZATION

The primary organizational plan of this lecture is to break down a topic by *listing* features of that topic. In this case, the lecture lists the eight principles underlying Amnesty International's work.

DEFINING VOCABULARY

The following words and expressions were used in the lecture that you just heard. You may remember the contexts in which you heard them. You will hear an additional example of each word or expression in a new context. After listening, write a definition for each word or expression.

1. abolition _____

2. death penalty _____

3. mandate _____

4. on behalf (of someone) _____

5. appeal _____

6. grounded in fact _____

7. credibility _____

8. concerted effort _____

9. economic sanctions _____

10. persuasion _____

11. impartiality _____

12. to pursue _____

13. ideology _____

14. sole _____

15. with no strings attached _____

16. relief funds _____

17. frontier _____

18. birthright _____

NOTE-TAKING PRACTICE

 Listen to the lecture a second time. Take notes using the following format. The comments in the left margin serve to remind you of the organization of the lecture.

introduction

list: principles
* underlying AI's*
* work*

Principles Underlying AI's Activities & Success:

principle 1

1.

principle 2

2.

principle 3

3.

principle 4

4.

principle 5

5.

principle 6

6.

principle 7

7.

principle 8

8.

conclusions

Review and revise your notes. Add information that you remember. If helpful, consider rewriting your notes. Make the relationship between ideas clear and make important ideas stand out.

POST-LECTURE READING AND DISCUSSION

Discuss the following in small groups.

1. Do you think Amnesty International serves an important purpose? Why or why not?

2. The following poem was written by Martin Niemoller, a German Protestant pastor (1892–1984). What does his poem mean to you?

> They came for the Communists, and I
>   didn't object—For I wasn't a Communist;
> They came for the Socialists, and I
>   didn't object—For I wasn't a Socialist;
> They came for the labor leaders, and I
>   didn't object—For I wasn't a labor leader;
> They came for the Jews, and I
>   didn't object—For I wasn't a Jew;
> Then they came for me—
> And there was no one left to object.

USING YOUR NOTES

Use your notes to answer the following questions.

1. Infer whether each statement is true or false. The lecturer does not explicitly make these statements. However, a thoughtful listener can draw conclusions from the lecture. Be prepared to support your answers.

_____ a. Amnesty International is an organization that works predominantly in the abstract sense (i.e., it focuses on large-scale, intangible, immaterial goals).

_____ b. Amnesty International feels that punishment of countries with bad human rights records is necessary.

_____ c. Amnesty International is basically a Western organization and is somewhat anti-Communist.

_____ d. Amnesty International publishes a "Ten Worst Countries for Human Rights" list every year.

2. Which of the following statements is Amnesty International likely to support? Check as many as are applicable. Be prepared to support your answers.

_____ a. It is better to focus on a limited area than to cover all the wrongs in the world.

_____ b. The strength of a group rests with its individual members.

_____ c. Change is brought about through military or economic pressure on a government.

_____ d. Taking swift action is more important than getting all the facts.

_____ e. It is important to set priorities, decide which countries are the worst in terms of human rights, and work there.

_____ f. We are all citizens of the world when it comes to involvement with human rights.

_____ g. Let's talk specifics, not abstractions.

_____ h. In order to change the world, you must start with yourself.

_____ i. If you are not part of the solution, you're part of the problem.

3. What is an Amnesty International adoption group?

_____

_____

4. How does Amnesty International ensure its impartiality? State at least two ways.

a. _____

b. _____

COMPARING IDEAS

1. In small groups, compare notes. What information do you have that your classmates don't? What information do they have that you don't?

2. In small groups, compare your answers to the preceding questions. If you have different answers, check your notes and discuss your reasons for making your choices.

3. Compare your rewritten notes to the sample rewritten notes in Appendix C. Notice the organization. Is yours similar or different? Are your notes equally effective in making important ideas stand out?

USING VOCABULARY

 You will hear vocabulary from this lecture in different contexts. Listen before reading each exercise. After listening, circle the letter of the closest paraphrase of the information that you heard.

1. a. The police held him, but no one hurt him.
   b. The police held him, but no one helped him.
   c. The police helped him, but no one else would.

2. a. Everyone except Mary voted for the new law.
   b. Everyone except Mary voted.
   c. Mary was the only one who voted.
   d. Mary voted in the same manner as everyone else did.

3. a. People in many parts of the world want the death penalty.
   b. People in many parts of the world are working to establish the death penalty.
   c. People in many parts of the world want to get rid of the death penalty.

4. a. People stopped trusting and believing the judge because she favored one side over another.
   b. People began to trust and believe the judge because she was fair to all sides.

5. a. He was honored because he prevented human rights abuses.
   b. He was detained because he permitted human rights abuses.
   c. He was executed because he permitted human rights abuses.

6. a. They tried to persuade the governor to kill the criminal.
   b. They tried to persuade the governor not to kill the criminal.

7. a. Someone gave money to the organization and expected nothing in return.
   b. Someone gave money to the organization but expected something in return.

8. a. Her father convinced her to give up her goals.
   b. Her father showed her how unrealistic her goals were.
   c. Her father convinced her to keep working toward her goals.
   d. Her father showed her how to keep working toward her goals.

RETAINING VOCABULARY

Write ten words from the lecture, reading, and discussion that you would like to remember. Use each word in an example that will remind you of its meaning.

Example

censor: The government tried to censor the press, but the newspaper published the articles anyway.

1. _____

_____

2. _____

_____

3. _____

_____

4. _____

_____

5. _____

_____

6. _____

_____

7. _____

_____

8. _____

_____

9. _____

_____

10. _____

_____

SPEAKING AND LISTENING ACTIVITY

A debate is an organized discussion involving two opposing views. The goal of a good debater is to present support for his or her own side as well as to counter arguments of his or her opponent.

Choose one of the following debate topics:

1. Internal Affairs and International Relations

   Team A: Human rights abuses are international issues that should be of concern to foreign governments, trade partners, and others in the international community.

   Team B: Human rights abuses are issues that should be handled internally without international interference.

or

2. Amnesty International's Principles

   Team A: Amnesty International's principles are the best means by which to deal with the problems of human rights violations.

   Team B: Amnesty International's principles need changing. There are more effective ways to deal with human rights violations.

Form two opposing teams, choosing three members for each team. Team members should meet to discuss ways to support their position. They should also discuss ways to counter the opposing team's arguments. One member is responsible for presenting the major arguments for the group's position. A second member is responsible for providing the counterargument. The third member is responsible for providing a final wrap-up and argument. Class members who are not speaking in the debate are responsible for noting the key points that each team makes.

The debate takes place in the following order:

1. Flip a coin to decide which team goes first.
2. The first team presents arguments to support its position. (5 min. maximum)
3. The second team presents arguments to support its position. (5 min. maximum)
4. The first team counters the second team's arguments. (3 min. maximum)
5. The second team counters the first team's arguments. (3 min. maximum)
6. The first team wraps up. (2 min. maximum)
7. The second team wraps up. (2 min. maximum)
8. At the end of the debate, the class votes for the winning team.

PRE-LECTURE DISCUSSION

Vocabulary
Related to Animal
Communication
and Pheromones

animal kingdom
nocturnal animal
aquatic animal
terrestrial animal

species

mammal
reptile
insect
amphibian
crustacean

primate
rodent

predator
prey

to migrate
to mate

hive
den
nest
lair

Additional
Vocabulary

Look at the pictures above. Do you know how ants communicate the location of food sources to other ants? How bees figure out the location of their particular bee colony? How snails mate and communicate the desire to mate to other snails? Do you know about any other types of animal communication systems? If so, describe them.

PREPARING FOR THE LECTURE

The title of the lecture is "Pheromones." Find a definition of *pheromone* in the dictionary. Based on this definition and the previous discussion questions, what do you expect the lecturer to talk about? Brainstorm ideas with your classmates.

LISTENING FOR THE LARGER PICTURE

Read the following questions before the lecture begins. Then, listen to the lecture once without taking notes. While listening, answer the questions.

1. The lecturer's goal is to tell the audience about pheromones. In order to do this, the lecturer (check as many as are correct):

    _____ a. defines the term *pheromone*.
    _____ b. shows the similarities and differences between pheromones and other forms of animal communication.
    _____ c. classifies the types of pheromones.
    _____ d. gives examples of different kinds of pheromones.
    _____ e. describes the chemical makeup of pheromones.

2. Which of the following are characteristics of pheromones? (Check as many as are appropriate.)

    _____ a. Pheromones may be detected by the sense of smell or taste.
    _____ b. Pheromones may be detected by any species nearby.
    _____ c. Pheromones are very sensitive and only require small amounts to get a response.
    _____ d. Pheromones may be detected by the sense of touch.
    _____ e. Pheromones must be produced in great quantities in order to be effective.
    _____ f. Each particular species is responsive only to its own species' pheromones.
    _____ g. The pheromones of one species have no effect on members of other species.

3. There are two types of pheromones: primer pheromones and releaser pheromones. How do they differ?

    _____

    _____

4. How many types of releaser pheromones does the speaker mention?

ORGANIZATION

The lecture primarily demonstrates three organizational plans: *defining a term*, *classifying*, and *exemplifying*. The lecturer defines *pheromone* by giving a simple definition and then expanding it by adding characteristics of pheromones. The lecturer then classifies pheromones into two types, primer and releaser pheromones, and further classifies releaser pheromones into four types, giving additional definitions and examples for each one.

DEFINING VOCABULARY

The following words and expressions were used in the lecture that you just heard. You may remember the contexts in which you heard them. You will hear an additional example of each word or expression in a new context. After listening, circle the letter of the definition that most closely matches what you think the word or expression means.

1. to emit
   a. to smell something
   b. to send out
   c. to take responsibility for

2. to evoke a response
   a. to respond (*to* someone else)
   b. to bring out a response (*from* someone else)
   c. to refuse to respond

3. physiological
   a. related to biological processes
   b. related to the mind
   c. related to the science of physics

4. mutually exclusive
   a. occurring together
   b. not occurring together
   c. exchanging basic parts

5. to disperse
   a. to separate and move into various directions
   b. to commit a crime; to perform an unlawful act
   c. to give an order; to command

6. to flee
   a. to burn; to burst into flames
   b. to live; to reside
   c. to run away; to escape

7. stimulant
   a. a substance that helps one sleep
   b. a substance that temporarily increases physiological activity
   c. a substance that one drinks

8. to arouse
   a. to scare away
   b. to excite
   c. to point out the direction

9. terrestrial
   a. related to land
   b. related to water
   c. related to air

10. navigational guide
    a. something that produces light
    b. something that contains water
    c. something that leads one on a particular path

11. to exhaust
    a. to increase the use of
    b. to use completely
    c. to continue the use of

12. insecticide
    a. a substance used to protect insects
    b. a substance used to kill insects
    c. a substance used to encourage insects to reproduce

NOTE-TAKING PRACTICE

 Listen to the lecture a second time. Take notes using the following format. The comments in the left margin serve to remind you of the organization of the lecture.

definition	Pheromones—
details about definition	
classifications	Types of pheromones:
definitions and examples	primer pheromone
	e.g.
	releaser pheromone
	alarm pheromone
	e.g.
	aggregation pheromone
	e.g.
	sex pheromone
	e.g.
	terrestrial trail pheromone
	e.g.
conclusions	

Review and revise your notes. Add information that you remember. If helpful, consider rewriting your notes. Make the relationship between ideas clear and make important ideas stand out.

POST-LECTURE READING AND DISCUSSION

Discuss the following in small groups.

1. The lecturer discusses pheromones and their function in the animal kingdom. However, the lecturer does not mention humans. Do you think humans are influenced by pheromones? If so, how?
2. Read the following article. Then discuss your answers to the questions that follow.

Researchers Sniff Out Pheromones

Gwenda Blair, *Los Angeles Times*

If the idea of using smell to find a mate sounds like a stretch, consider a further stretch: pheromones, long-sought odorless but gender-specific chemical signals exchanged by most mammals but until recently believed to be extinct in humans.

A few years ago, Dr. Louis Monti-Bloch, a physiologist at the University of Utah, teamed up with Dr. David Berliner, a former anatomist, and tested what they believed were human pheromones on volunteers. They reported that these elicited an electrical response in two small, vestigial pits near the volunteers' nostrils—presumably, the pheromone receptors. Further, Berliner claimed, responses to pheromones were gender-specific. Unlike odors, which almost always affect women more than men, pheromones evoked an equally strong reaction in men and women.

Berliner promptly patented these substances and founded a company called Erox to manufacture them. Most of the scientific establishment remains skeptical, however. For one thing, says Michael Meredith, a biologist at Florida State University, Berliner and Monti-Bloch's work has not been replicated. And Berliner's haste to make a profit from his research seems, well, unseemly to his peers.

Yet supporting evidence is slowly accumulating. For example, Martha McClintock, a biopsychologist at the University of Chicago, confirmed that a group of women living together in a college dormitory tend to synchronize menstrual cycles, which many consider a pheromonal effect. Researchers from the University of Bern, Switzerland, found that when women were asked to choose among T-shirts worn by men who were strangers, they mysteriously selected those of men whose immune systems, according to DNA analyses, were most unlike their own— possible evidence of a built-in smell-based preference for mates who could help produce offspring with wide immunological coverage, researchers speculated.

The upshot: Don't spend any money on a pheromonal spritz, but if you're attracted to a stranger's T-shirt, don't assume it's the logo you like.

a. How many research studies are discussed in this article? What did each research study find?
b. Why are Berliner's peers skeptical of his work?
c. Does this article support the idea that pheromones are extinct in humans?
d. In some magazines, you might see advertisements that offer pheromone-based lotions which are supposed to attract members of the opposite sex. Based on the information in the article, would you believe these claims? Why or why not? Would you purchase a lotion like this? Why or why not?

USING YOUR NOTES

Use your notes to answer the following questions.

1. Define the term *pheromone* as used in the lecture.

_____

_____

2. True or False?
    _____ a. Pheromones are used by a variety of species ranging from one-celled animals to higher primates (i.e., an order including monkeys, apes, and humans).
    _____ b. When an animal releases a pheromone that calls other animals to attack, this is an example of a primer pheromone.
    _____ c. When a female snail releases a pheromone that causes a sexually undifferentiated snail to develop into a male, this is an example of a primer pheromone.
    _____ d. Primer pheromones cause psychological changes.
    _____ e. Bees find their way back to their hives because of terrestrial trail pheromones.
    _____ f. Pheromones can be used to control animal behavior for crop protection.
    _____ g. Pheromones can harm people who eat crops grown near to where the pheromones were used.
    _____ h. The four types of releaser pheromones are mutually exclusive.

3. Pheromones are said to be highly sensitive and highly specific. Explain these concepts.

_____

_____

4. Contrast the terms *primer pheromone* and *releaser pheromone*.

_____

_____

_____

5. In a paragraph, discuss the different types of releaser pheromones in terms of their functions. Give an example of how each pheromone type can be observed in the animal kingdom.

_____

_____

_____

_____

_____

_____

_____

COMPARING IDEAS

1. In small groups, compare notes. What information do you have that your classmates don't? What information do they have that you don't?

2. In small groups, compare your answers to the preceding questions. If you have different answers, check your notes and discuss your reasons for making your choices.

3. Compare your rewritten notes to the sample rewritten notes in Appendix C. Notice the organization. Is yours similar or different? Are your notes equally effective in making important ideas stand out?

USING VOCABULARY

You will hear vocabulary from this lecture in different contexts. Listen before reading each exercise. After listening, fill in the blanks with words from the vocabulary list to paraphrase the information that you heard. (You may change the verb forms and tenses.)

1. *stimulants   insecticides   navigational guides   physiological changes*

   Workers at the chemical company complained of stomach pains. Examinations of the chemicals that they were using did, in fact, demonstrate that they acted as _____, causing _____ in subjects.

2. *to flee   to emit   to disperse   to evoke a response   to exhaust*

   The refugees were forced to _____ their homeland. Because it was dangerous to leave in groups, large families had to _____ in the hope that they would join together again in a new country. The situation of these refugees _____ throughout the world, and offers of help came from far and wide.

3. *navigational guide   to emit   to exhaust   to arouse   to flee*

   The hikers were lost in the mountains and worried. Their flashlights were only _____ a faint light. They had almost completely _____ their food supply. They tried using a compass as a _____, and hoped that this would lead them back to the road and safety. They finally made it. Their story of walking twenty miles in the semidarkness and with little food _____ the curiosity and interest of the public, and many news articles were written about their days in the woods.

4. *physiological changes   insecticides   stimulants   terrestrial*

   The _____ worked well on _____ insects but did not work as well on water-based insects.

RETAINING VOCABULARY

Write ten words from the lecture, reading, and discussion that you would like to remember. Use each word in an example that will remind you of its meaning.

Example

emit: Cars emit chemicals that cause air pollution.

1. _____

_____

2. _____

_____

3. _____

_____

4. _____

_____

5. _____

_____

6. _____

_____

7. _____

_____

8. _____

_____

9. _____

_____

10. _____

_____

WRITING ACTIVITY

Work in small groups to write a promotional brochure for a pheromone-based lotion, perfume, or cologne. Consider your target audience and what would encourage them to buy the product. Think of a catchy name to draw their attention. How much would you charge for a thirty-day supply?

PRE-LECTURE READING AND DISCUSSION

Vocabulary
Related to
Astronomy and
Space Travel

astronomy
astronaut

space station
space shuttle

manned/unmanned
  mission

rocket

satellite

to launch

to orbit

galaxy
Milky Way

stellar
lunar
solar
celestial
terrestrial

phases of the moon

extraterrestrial life

Additional
Vocabulary

How do you think the experience of seeing the Earth from space changes a person's perceptions or way of thinking? Discuss your ideas in small groups and summarize them below.

_____

_____

_____

_____

When you have reached some conclusions, read the following quotes from astronauts who have been in space. What key changes in perception do these astronauts express? Were your impressions similar to theirs?

> *We are passing over the Himalayas. We can see the mountain ranges with the highest peaks in the world. At the end of the Kathmandu valley . . . I found Everest. How many people dream of conquering Everest, so that they can look down from it, and yet for us from above, it was difficult even to locate it.*
>
> **—Valentin Lebedev (former USSR)**

> *The first day or so we all pointed to our countries. The third or fourth day we were pointing to our continents. By the fifth day we were aware of only one Earth.*
>
> **—Sultan Bin Salman al-Saud (Saudi Arabia)**

> *I have been in love with the sky since birth. And when I could fly, I wanted to go higher, to enter space and become a "man of the heights." During the eight days I spent in space, I realized that mankind needs height primarily to better know our long-suffering Earth, to see what cannot be seen close up. Not just to love her beauty, but also to ensure that we do not bring even the slightest harm to the natural world.*
>
> **—Pham Tuan (Vietnam)**

We went to the moon as technicians; we returned as humanitarians.
—**Edgar Mitchell** *(USA)*

It isn't important in which sea or lake you observe a slick of pollution, or in the forests of which country a fire breaks out, or on which continent a hurricane arises. You are standing guard over the whole of our Earth.
—**Yuri Artyukin** *(former USSR)*

Under a full moon the clouds are luminous in pearly reflection. The high-altitude atmospheric airglow appears on the horizon as a stunning bronze-colored band above the now dark air. And lightning presents a show of beauty and power as it illuminates billowing clouds and weather fronts sometimes for distances of tens of miles. Beneath this natural wonder cities glow yellow or white, but are diminutive in scale.
—**Charles Walker** *(USA)*

PREPARING FOR THE LECTURE

The title of the lecture is "The Near Side of the Moon." What do you know about the moon? What would you like to learn about it? What do you expect the lecturer to talk about? Brainstorm ideas with your classmates.

LISTENING FOR THE LARGER PICTURE

Read the following questions before the lecture begins. Then, listen to the lecture once without taking notes. After listening, answer the questions.

1. The primary purpose of the lecture is to _____
   _____ .

2. What are the two major types of surfaces of the near side of the moon?

   a. _____   b. _____

   Which major type of surface is characterized as follows? Write *a* or *b* in each of the spaces.

   ____ fairly smooth

   ____ dominated by craters

   ____ made of valleys and basins filled with molten lava

   ____ contain areas of high concentration of mass (mascon)

   ____ appear as the lighter and brighter parts of photographs of the moon

   Look at the photo of the near side of the moon on page 124. Label each of the surface types.

3. In addition to discussing the geographic features of the moon (i.e., land formations) and the issue of water on the moon, the lecturer discusses two other major characteristics of the near side of the moon. What are they?

   a. _____   b. _____

ORGANIZATION

The lecture primarily *describes* an object by *listing* different features. While doing this, the lecturer *compares and contrasts* the moon's surface and the Earth's surfaces, *classifies* the surface types of the moon, and *defines* new terms.

DEFINING VOCABULARY

 The following words and expressions were used in the lecture that you just heard. You may remember the contexts in which you heard them. You will hear an additional example of each word or expression in a new context. After listening, circle the letter of the definition that most closely matches what you think the word or expression means.

1. firsthand knowledge
   a. something learned through direct experience
   b. something learned through reading or hearing about another person's experience
   c. something learned before other information

2. perpetually
   a. lasting forever
   b. occurring seasonally
   c. occurring frequently

3. molten lava
   a. a volcano
   b. colored streams of water
   c. melted rock coming from a break in a planet's surface

4. to dominate
   a. to exist in large numbers or as a major feature
   b. to exist in small numbers or as a minor feature
   c. to not exist at all

5. unanimous
   a. in complete agreement
   b. having unknown views
   c. in complete disagreement

6. to be devoid (of something)
   a. to have relatively few
   b. to avoid
   c. to have none

7. to moderate
   a. to make something less extreme
   b. to make something warmer
   c. to make something colder

8. twilight
   a. direct sunlight occurring around noon
   b. the period of time during which the sky is lit, but the sun has not yet *risen* over the horizon
   c. the period of time during which the sky is lit, but the sun has already *set* below the horizon

9. dawn
   a. direct sunlight occurring around noon
   b. the period of time during which the sky is lit, but the sun has not yet *risen* over the horizon
   c. the period of time during which the sky is lit, but the sun has already *set* below the horizon

10. to attribute
    a. to regard as the cause
    b. to regard as similar
    c. to regard as unrelated

11. slim chance
    a. no possibility
    b. low probability
    c. good possibility

NOTE-TAKING PRACTICE

 Listen to the lecture a second time. Take notes using the following format. The comments in the left margin serve to remind you of the organization of the lecture.

introduction	
feature 1: geographic features	Surface features of near side of moon — side perpetually turned to earth
	lowlands (maria/mare) + highlands
classification of surfaces	
description of each type	
feature 2: water issue	
feature 3: temperature	
feature 4: light	
conclusions	

Review and revise your notes. Add information that you remember. If helpful, consider rewriting your notes. Make the relationship between ideas clear and make important ideas stand out.

POST-LECTURE READING AND DISCUSSION

Discuss the following in small groups.

1. Read the article below. Then discuss your answers to the questions that follow.

Moon Rooms?

Jeannye Thornton, *U.S. News and World Report*

In a 1967 address to the American Astronautical Society, hotelier Barron Hilton invited his audience to imagine moonbound tourists traveling by space ferry to a Lunar Hilton with 100 guest rooms and a dining room serving everything from reconstituted martinis to freeze-dried steaks.

Hilton International Hotels is keeping Barron Hilton's moon dream alive. The Britain-based chain recently hired British architect Peter Inston to design a lunar hotel. Inston says he has been talking with NASA, university, and independent space scientists about the viability of a resort on the moon. Hilton International has spent about $300,000 so far to explore building a glass-domed inn with thousands of pressurized guest rooms, galactic viewing platforms, and a medical center.

Is this just a Hilton International publicity stunt? Skeptics point out the huge costs, complex engineering challenges, and potential safety risks. But Professor Richard S. Ellis, director of the Institute of Astronomy at Cambridge University in England, told London's *Sunday Times* he considers the project "perfectly feasible." It will eventually come to pass, Ellis predicted, if only to meet tourist demand for exotic places to visit.

a. What does Barron Hilton do for a living?
b. What is his "moon dream"?
c. What is Hilton International Hotels doing to keep his dream "alive"?
d. How are people reacting to Hilton International Hotel's actions?

2. *According to a survey conducted by the Space Transportation Association, a private organization, the average person would pay two months' salary for the opportunity to travel in space.*

—Los Angeles Times, 6/23/98

Would you travel into space if given the opportunity? How much would you pay if the opportunity were offered to the highest bidder?

USING YOUR NOTES

Use your notes to answer the following questions.

1. How does the lecturer define the terms below?

    a. maria _____

    b. mare _____

    c. mascon _____

2. Write the characteristics of the two surface types on the near side of the moon.

    a. _____

    b. _____

3. The lecturer mentions three consequences of the lack of atmosphere on the moon. Discuss those consequences and explain why the lack of atmosphere causes these effects.

    a. _____

    _____

    b. _____

    _____

    c. _____

    _____

4. According to the lecturer, why is the possibility of ice crystals on the moon so important?

    _____ a. The crystals could be used as a source of drinking water.

    _____ b. It suggests that there is, in fact, an atmosphere on the moon.

    _____ c. The crystals could eventually provide components for rocket fuel.

    _____ d. all of the above

    _____ e. none of the above

5. What is the temperature range on the near side of the moon?

    _____

COMPARING IDEAS

1. In small groups, compare notes. What information do you have that your classmates don't? What information do they have that you don't?

2. In small groups, compare your answers to the preceding questions. If you have different answers, check your notes and discuss your reasons for making your choices.

3. Compare your rewritten notes to the sample rewritten notes in Appendix C. Notice the organization. Is yours similar or different? Are your notes equally effective in making important ideas stand out?

USING VOCABULARY

 You will hear vocabulary from the lecture in different contexts. Listen before reading each exercise. After listening, circle the letter of the closest paraphrase of the information that you heard.

1. a. In January 1977, Voyager 2 was sent into space.
   b. In January 1977, Voyager 2 got lost.
   c. In January 1977, Voyager 2 was built.

2. a. Photographs of Ariel, one of Uranus's moons, taken by Voyager 2 in 1986, show that it has some valleys and canyons.
   b. Photographs of Ariel, one of Uranus's moons, taken by Voyager 2 in 1986, show that its major feature is its valleys and canyons.
   c. Photographs of Ariel, one of Uranus's moons, taken by Voyager 2 in 1986, show that it has absolutely no valleys or canyons.

3. a. Right now (and for the next forty years or so), there is constant sunlight at Uranus's south pole.
   b. Right now (and for the next forty years or so), there is no sunlight at Uranus's south pole.

4. a. Scientists suggest a possible cause for this phenomenon.[1]
   b. Scientists suggest a possible result for this phenomenon.
   c. Scientists have little idea about what causes this phenomenon.

5. a. Uranus's atmosphere consists of hydrogen, helium, methane, and oxygen.
   b. Uranus's atmosphere consists of hydrogen, helium, and methane.

RETAINING VOCABULARY

Write ten words from the lecture, article, and discussion that you would like to remember. Use each word in an example that will remind you of its meaning.

Example

launch: The space shuttle Challenger exploded a few minutes after being launched.

1. _____

_____

---

[1] **phenomemon:** an unusual or significant event

2. _____
   _____

3. _____
   _____

4. _____
   _____

5. _____
   _____

6. _____
   _____

7. _____
   _____

8. _____
   _____

9. _____
   _____

10. _____
    _____

SPEAKING AND LISTENING ACTIVITY

The Hilton International Hotel moon hotel design team is exploring building a "glass-domed inn with thousands of pressurized guest rooms, galactic viewing platforms, and a medical center." Work in small groups to design a moon hotel. Take into account the features of the moon as presented in the lecture (e.g., temperature, water, land features, light). Where would you build the hotel? What would it look like? What amenities would it offer? What features should be emphasized to encourage people to visit? Use your imagination. When you finish, present your plan to your classmates.

PRE-LECTURE DISCUSSION

Vocabulary
Related to Health
and Diet

nutrition
nutritional value

diet

malnutrition
starvation

life expectancy

health hazard
side effect
birth defect

carcinogen
carcinogenic

additive
preservative
food supplement

processed food

Additional
Vocabulary

Discuss your answers to the following questions in small groups.

1. What did you have for dinner last night? What did you eat that was good for you? What did you eat that wasn't good for you?

2. How much coffee or tea do you consume each day? If you drink tea, what kind of tea do you drink—herbal tea, black tea, green tea, oolong tea? Do you think you should increase or decrease your intake of any of these drinks? Why?

3. How concerned are you about the nutritional value of the food you eat? Do you buy organic fruits and vegetables? Do you try to avoid fried foods? Do you read the labels on food products? Do you avoid foods with preservatives or chemical additives in them?

4. Do you know of any foods that have disease-fighting properties? If so, what are they?

PREPARING FOR THE LECTURE

The title of the lecture is "Drink Your Green Tea!" What do you expect the lecturer to talk about? Brainstorm ideas with your classmates.

LISTENING FOR THE LARGER PICTURE

 Read the following sentences before the lecture begins. Then, listen to the lecture once without taking notes. After listening, circle the letters of the sentences that describe what the lecturer does.

   a. provides evidence to support the idea that "drinking green tea is good for people"
   b. provides evidence to support the idea that "drinking green tea is hazardous to one's health"
   c. talks about three different kinds of tea
   d. talks about four different kinds of tea
   e. describes the different processes used to manufacture each of the different kinds of tea
   f. describes the process of brewing a good cup of tea

ORGANIZATION

The lecture demonstrates three different organizational plans: *describing a process*, *classifying*, and *making a generalization and providing evidence for that generalization*. The lecturer begins by talking about the different types of tea. Then, the lecturer describes (and occasionally contrasts) the different processes for manufacturing those different types (including discussing the role of fermentation[1] in the process). Finally, the lecturer provides evidence for the idea that "green tea is good for you."

DEFINING VOCABULARY

 The following words and expressions were used in the lecture that you just heard. You may remember the contexts in which you heard them. You will hear an additional example of each word or expression in a new context. After listening, circle the letter of the definition that most closely matches what you think the word or expression means.

   1. to hold in high esteem
      a. to dislike and disdain
      b. to respect and admire greatly
      c. to be unavailable or exist in limited quantities

---

[1] **to ferment:** to change chemically when a substance causes complex organic compounds to split into relatively simple substances (e.g., yeast causes sugar to change to alcohol and carbon dioxide)

2. steam
  a. wrinkled clothing
  b. a small body of water (e.g., a pond)
  c. water in the form of a gas

3. to roll
  a. to prepare something sweet (e.g., a cake or pie)
  b. to move a boat through water
  c. to spread out flat and thin by using a tube-shaped object

4. humid
  a. dry (air or weather)
  b. hot (air or weather)
  c. damp (air or weather)

5. to wither
  a. to become smaller, less colorful, or less fresh
  b. to smell good
  c. to grow and produce blossoms

6. incidence
  a. disappearance
  b. unusual nature
  c. rate of occurrence

7. to isolate
  a. to keep apart; to separate from others
  b. to make animals (especially horses) sick
  c. to cool to almost freezing

8. to inhibit
  a. to hold back; to prevent
  b. to live in a place; to reside
  c. to move from one place to another

9. toxicity
  a. movement in and around
  b. growth of life
  c. level of poison

10. stimulant
  a. a substance that is heated and drunk
  b. a substance that gives energy or encourages activity
  c. a substance that decreases energy or discourages activity

In addition to these words, the lecturer also uses a number of terms for different diseases related to various parts of the body. Check the meanings of the following medical terms: *lung cancer, stomach cancer, esophageal cancer* (or cancer of the esophagus), *cholesterol, tumor, dental cavity.*

NOTE-TAKING PRACTICE

Listen to the lecture a second time. Take notes using the following format. The comments in the left margin serve to remind you of the organization of the lecture.

introduction

classification and
    contrast of types of
    tea

generalization

    evidence for
        generalization

Green tea is good for you!

—

—

—

—

continuing research on
    green tea

conclusions

Review and revise your notes. Add information that you remember. If helpful, consider rewriting your notes. Make the relationship between ideas clear and make important ideas stand out.

POST-LECTURE READING AND DISCUSSION

It is important to read and listen critically. For example, this lecture reports on health benefits found to be associated with green tea. Is this information certain? Are there reasons to question this information? Read the following excerpt from an article in the *Tufts University Diet and Nutrition Letter*. Then discuss your answers to the questions that follow in small groups.

Reading Tea Leaves for Health Benefits

To date there have been no human studies in which people have been given tea and then observed to see if they develop cancers at a lower rate than others. There have, however, been almost 100 epidemiologic studies in which, for example, people who have cancer are asked how much tea they commonly drank during their lifetimes and then compared to people without cancer to see if the tea drinking levels between the two groups differed. Unfortunately, epidemiologic evidence is often relatively murky. People might not remember accurately enough their tea consumption patterns over several decades. And even if they do, it doesn't prove that tea and not something else about their lifestyles is what affected their risk of cancer.

To make matters more complicated, the results of epidemiologic research on tea have been mixed. In some studies, tea appeared protective. In others, it seemed to make no difference. And in still others, people who drank more tea actually came down with more cases of cancer.

But researchers are not deterred. They feel the results vary because the studies have not been well controlled. For instance, if tea drinkers in a particular study don't have fewer cases of cancer than non-tea drinkers, it might be because they smoked or drank too much alcohol and that those lifestyle habits overpowered the beneficial effects of tea but were not accounted for. On the flip side, if the cancer rates in a set of tea drinkers appear almost too low to be true, it could be that the subjects also ate diets low in fat or high in vegetables and fruits, both of which inhibit certain kinds of tumors.

To shed light on the matter in a more thorough and consistent way, the chief executive officer of the International Epidemiology Institute in Maryland, William Blot, M.D., says, "We need more and better controlled investigations in humans." And he believes such investigations are worth conducting. The evidence from studies thus far is encouraging enough, he says, to "provide incentive for additional research to understand the role of tea drinking in a healthy diet."

Dr. Mukhtar, the skin cancer researcher at Case Western Reserve, agrees. He says that by giving tea to a high-risk group of people, such as those who have skin cancers removed yearly, a lot could be learned about its ability to protect against sun-caused tumors. That would be much more telling than asking people who already have cancer how much tea they used to drink. Once tea's efficacy is proven, which Dr. Mukhtar believes is only a matter of time, he expects to see its active ingredients incorporated into suntan lotions, over-the-counter cosmetics, even shampoos.

Of course, no matter what might eventually be confirmed about the benefits of tea, switching from, say, coffee to tea is never going to take the place of eating a relatively low-fat diet with plenty of vegetables, fruits, and whole grains, nor is it going to replace engaging several days a week in vigorous physical activity. Like oat bran, tea is just one food that, included in a lifestyle that's healthful overall, may provide a bit of an edge in staving off chronic diseases of aging.

1. According to this article, what concerns should people have about studies claiming that green tea improves health?
2. According to this article, what types of studies need to be done?
3. What conclusions do you think the author of the article wants you to reach about health regarding tea?
4. Do you plan to change any of your personal habits based on information you heard in the lecture or read in this article? If so, what do you plan to do? If not, why not?

USING YOUR NOTES

Use your notes to answer the following questions.

1. True or False?
   _____ a. All tea comes from the same plant group.
   _____ b. Oolong tea is the least processed of all the different types of tea.
   _____ c. Black tea turns black because it is burned.
   _____ d. About 75 percent of world tea production is black tea.
   _____ e. The studies showing reduction in cancer of the esophagus were done in Japan.
   _____ f. A cup of green tea contains more vitamin C than a cup of orange juice.
   _____ g. A research team in the United States found a substance in green tea that may help protect against dental cavities.
   _____ h. Green tea contains the same amount of caffeine as coffee and black tea.

2. According to Japanese research, drinkers of green tea have lower rates of which of the following? (Check all answers that apply.)
   _____ a. cancer of the esophagus
   _____ b. stomach cancer
   _____ c. depression
   _____ d. skin tumors
   _____ e. blood cholesterol
   _____ f. breast cancer
   _____ g. lung cancer

3. What are the steps to process and produce green tea?

   _____

   _____

   _____

4. What are the steps to process and produce black tea?

   _____

   _____

   _____

5. The Designer Food Program of the National Institute of Health is research-ing forty foods that have unusually powerful disease-fighting abilities. What does it hope to do with this information?

_____

_____

_____

COMPARING IDEAS

1. In small groups, compare notes. What information do you have that your classmates don't? What information do they have that you don't?

2. In small groups, compare your answers to the preceding questions. If you have different answers, check your notes and discuss your reasons for mak-ing your choices.

3. Compare your rewritten notes to the sample rewritten notes in Appendix C. Notice the organization. Is yours similar or different? Are your notes equally effective in making important ideas stand out?

USING VOCABULARY

 You will hear vocabulary from the lecture and discussion in different contexts. After listening, circle the letter of the closest paraphrase of the information that you heard.

1. a. In many countries, people are living longer because they are losing weight.
   b. In many countries, people are living longer because they eat healthier.
   c. In many countires, more and more people expect to improve their eating habits.

2. a. The doctor irons all of her clothes for work.
   b. The doctor's professional rates are very high.
   c. The doctor is respected for her work.

3. a. People can take as many vitamins as they want without negative side effects.
   b. It is possible to suffer negative side effects from vitamins if taken in high doses.
   c. Vitamins rarely work unless taken in great quantities.

4. a. The factory is respected for its work in improving the environment.
   b. The factory is emitting cancer-causing substances into the environment.
   c. The factory produces respected drugs that are known to reduce the inci-dence of cancer.

5. a. In the Pacific, there is an island that is very distant from other places and has a very quickly growing birth rate.
   b. In the Pacific, there is an island that is very distant from other places and has an unusually high number of babies born with health problems.
   c. In the Pacific, there is a group of islands where few babies are being born.

RETAINING VOCABULARY

Write ten words from the lecture, reading, and discussion that you would like to remember. Use each word in an example that will remind you of its meaning.

Example

additive: People should read food labels so that they can see whether their food is natural or whether it contains lots of chemical additives.

1. _____
   _____

2. _____
   _____

3. _____
   _____

4. _____
   _____

5. _____
   _____

6. _____
   _____

7. _____
   _____

8. _____
   _____

9. _____
   _____

10. _____
    _____

WRITING ACTIVITY

Read an article from the library or the Internet about a food, herb, or vitamin and its reported health benefits. Summarize the key points of your article in a paragraph. Publish your findings in a class newsletter. Be sure to include references to the original articles.

Vocabulary
Related to Voting
and Voter Turnout

candidate
nominee
to nominate

party

primary

campaign

party platform

ballot
absentee ballot

to cast a ballot
to go to the polls

voting booth
polling place

to run for office
in the running

to drop out of the race

apathy
alienation
disillusionment
mistrust

Additional
Vocabulary

PRE-LECTURE DISCUSSION

Discuss the following chart in small groups.

1. The chart reports participation in presidential elections from 1972 to 1996. Using these statistics, draw conclusions about trends in voting and not voting. Then answer the questions that follow.

Percentage Reporting Registering or Voting[a] in U.S. Elections, 1972 to 1996

Presidential Election Year	% of People Reporting They Registered	% of People Reporting They Voted
1972	72.3	63.0
1976	66.7	59.2
1980	66.9	59.2
1984	68.3	59.9
1988	66.6	57.4
1992	68.2	61.3
1996	65.9	54.2

Source: U.S. Bureau of the Census

[a] Note that the number of people reporting registering and voting is higher than the number of people who actually registered and voted.

Group's conclusions:

_____

_____

_____

_____

_____

_____

2. Look at the following chart reporting participation in the 1996 American presidential election. Percentages are listed according to sex, racial and ethnic group, education, and age. Using these statistics, draw conclusions about tendencies of groups to register, vote, and not vote.

Characteristics of Voting Age Population Who Reported Registering or Voting (for any office or issue on ballot), November 1996

Characteristics	% of People Reporting They Registered	% of People Reporting They Voted
Sex:		
Female	67.3	55.5
Male	64.4	52.8
Race and Ethnicity:		
Black	63.5	50.6
Spanish origin[b]	35.7	26.7
White	67.7	56.0
Education:		
Less than high school	40.7	29.9
Some high school	47.9	33.8
High school graduate	62.2	49.1
Some college (including Associate Degree)	72.9	60.5
Bachelor's Degree or higher	80.4	72.6
Age:		
18–24 years old	48.8	32.4
25–44 years old	61.9	49.2
45–64 years old	73.5	64.4
65+ years old	77.0	67.0

Source: U.S. Bureau of the Census

[b] Persons of Spanish origin may be of any race.

Group's conclusions:

_____

_____

_____

_____

_____

_____

3. Discuss your answers to the following questions.

   a. Are you surprised by the conclusions of these statistics? Why or why not?
   b. Why do you think certain groups in the United States vote less frequently than others?
   c. Why do you think the U.S. population as a whole votes and registers in such small numbers?
   d. Do you vote regularly? If so, why? If not, why not?

PREPARING FOR THE LECTURE

The title of the lecture is "Voter Turnout in the United States" What do you expect the lecturer to talk about? Brainstorm ideas with your classmates.

LISTENING FOR THE LARGER PICTURE

Read the following summary before the lecture begins. Then, listen to the lecture once without taking notes. While listening, fill in the blanks.

1. The lecturer introduces the topic by providing background information about the history of _____ in the United States.

2. The lecturer focuses on the causes of _____ .

3. The lecturer classifies _____ into two types: _____ and _____ . Then, the lecturer gives examples of each of these types.

4. The lecturer lists the results of a poll asking why _____ and lists the characteristics of voters and nonvoters.

5. Based on this study and others, the lecturer states that a general trend seems to be that the _____ , _____ , and _____ are seriously underrepresented in the voting booth and that this pattern is not accidental.

6. The lecturer concludes by giving reasons why the picture is not as bleak as it first appears—because _____ and _____ . The lecturer ends by showing some optimism about the future.

ORGANIZATION

The lecture primarily demonstrates two organizational plans: *describing a causal relationship* (the causes of low voter turnout) and *listing* (the results of a poll and the characteristics of nonvoters). In order to describe the causes of low voter turnout, the lecturer organizes supporting ideas in a number of ways: *classifying* and *exemplifying* (the types of obstacles to voting), and also *comparing and contrasting* (voter and nonvoter characteristics).

DEFINING VOCABULARY

The following words and expressions were used in the lecture that you just heard. You may remember the contexts in which you heard them. You will hear an additional example of each word or expression in a new context. After listening, use context clues to write a definition for each word or expression.

1. time-consuming _____

2. obstacle _____

3. explicit _____

4. respondent _____

5. regardless (of something) _____

6. ethnicity _____

7. status _____

8. trend _____

9. bleak _____

NOTE-TAKING PRACTICE

Listen to the lecture a second time. Take notes using the following format. The comments in the left margin serve to remind you of the organization of the lecture.

introduction	
causes	Causes of Low Voter Turnout?
	Not apathy
classification of causes	INSTITUTIONAL REASONS + POLITICAL REASONS
examples of each classification	
list of poll results	Results of poll asking why people didn't vote

list of characteristics of voters/nonvoters	Voter/nonvoter characteristics
conclusions from nonvoter characteristics	Trend
conclusions from entire lecture	Conclusions

Review and revise your notes. Add information that you remember. If helpful, consider rewriting your notes. Make the relationship between ideas clear and make important ideas stand out.

POST-LECTURE READING AND DISCUSSION

Discuss the following in small groups.

1. Refer to the conclusions that your group drew from the charts on pages 140 and 141. Did the lecture confirm or refute your conclusions? What voting trends do you expect in the future? Why?

2. Some political scientists and mathematicians blame the low voter turnout on the U.S. election system. Read the following article. Then discuss your answers to the following questions.

   a. How many different types of voting systems are mentioned in the article? What are they? How do they work?
   b. Which system is generally used in the United States? According to the article, what problems are associated with it?
   c. What voting systems are used in countries with which you are familiar? What are the pros and cons of those systems?

Vetoing the Way America Votes

K.C. Cole, *Los Angeles Times*

Blame electoral woes on how we pick our leaders, mathematicians say. Dumping winner-take-all pluralities could ease apathy, extremism and mudslinging, they add.

Negative campaigning, low voter turnout, elections polarized by such issues as race and abortion—such all-too-familiar ills appear more and more frequently as blotches on the face of American democracy.

But a widely overlooked factor in the elections equation—the mathematics of voting itself—could have the power to at least alleviate, if not cure, these ills, according to political scientists and mathematicians who have studied the intricacies of voting systems.

In a country where people vote on just about everything—from presidents to prom queens—remarkably little attention is paid to the underlying rules of voting. Most Americans take for granted that the "winner takes all" system used in most U.S. elections is sacred. To the extent that they think about the system at all, people assume that as long as the process of voting is fair, the outcome will represent the wishes of most people, most of the time.

Mathematicians know differently. In fact, for more than 200 years, they have been studying the flaws of voting systems and arguing about which is the least harmful. The subject is well known in academic circles. In 1951, economist Kenneth Arrow proved mathematically that no democratic voting system can be completely fair (and won the Nobel prize for his efforts). This notion is known as "Arrow's impossibility theorem" because it proves that perfect democracy is impossible.

"Every system has something wrong with it," said Temple University mathematician John Allen Paulos, "but some work better more

often." Mathematicians do not agree on the best system. But they have no problem pointing their fingers at the worst: the plurality system used in most U.S. elections.

The issue is of more than academic interest. Plurality systems hand victory to the candidate with the most votes even if that candidate falls far short of a majority and even if the candidate is the person the majority likes least. The current systems can encourage extremism, reward name-calling, alienate voters and fail to reflect the wishes of most of the people much of the time.

The experts disagree about which alternative system is best. Some, for example, argue for approval voting, which allows everyone to cast one vote per candidate—changing the "one person, one vote" dictum to "one candidate, one vote." The candidate thus "approved of" by the most voters wins. While plurality systems encourage candidates to take extreme positions that develop a hard core of support, approval voting requires candidates to appeal for broad support. The system, experts believe, might do a lot to eliminate negative campaigning. "You would want to get at least partial approval from supporters of your opposition," Steven Brams, political scientist and mathematician, said. Approval voting would also help minority candidates. "Minorities can't be ignored because majority candidates need their support to win."

Approval voting is not without its detractors, however. Paulos argues that it tends to produce bland, mediocre winners. "Someone who doesn't have any sharp edges won't turn people off," he said. "But sometimes you

want someone who polarizes people because one of the poles is right."

The system Paulos likes much better is cumulative voting, in which voters can pile up several votes for a single candidate they feel strongly about. As in approval voting, each voter has as many votes as candidates and can distribute those votes among the candidates or give them all to one candidate. "It's a good way to give minorities a voice," said Paulos. "Any group that has sufficient cohesion to vote as a bloc can win."

Robert Richie, the director of the Center for Voting and Democracy, favors a system called preference voting—also known as the transferable ballot. Under preference voting, each voter ranks each candidate first, second, third, and so forth. But if after an initial count, someone's first-place choice seems doomed to defeat, then that voter's second-place vote is counted instead. While preference voting may sound complicated, Richie said it is used in other countries without problems and generates far better voter turnouts than in the U.S. It is used to choose the five nominees in each Academy Award category—a fact that should vouch for its simplicity, he argued. "It's not any harder than learning the rules of baseball or basketball," Richie said.

In the end, deciding on the fairest voting system will probably come down to, well, voting. "Before you decide on the substance, you have to decide what voting method you're going to use," said Paulos. "And then, what method are we going to use to choose the method? It can get all tangled and awful."

USING YOUR NOTES

Use your notes to answer the following questions.

1. Describe the relationship between voting patterns and each of the following factors.

   a. education _____

   _____

   b. income _____

   _____

   c. age _____

   _____

   d. sex _____

   _____

   e. race or ethnicity _____

   _____

2. In the poll that asked why people didn't vote,

   a. what percentage answered that they didn't register? _____

   b. what percentage gave explicitly political reasons for not voting? _____

3. Give one example of an institutional reason for not voting.

   _____

4. Give one example of a political reason for not voting.

   _____

5. True or False?

   _____ a. As educational level rises, the likelihood that a person will vote goes up regardless of race or ethnicity.

   _____ b. There are primarily three types of reasons for not voting: institutional reasons, political reasons, and personal reasons.

   _____ c. Those with higher-status jobs are more likely to vote than those with lower-status jobs.

   _____ d. The primary reason for not voting is simply apathy.

   _____ e. According to the lecturer, the institutional obstacles to voting are more difficult to change than the political obstacles.

   _____ f. The lecturer believes that the increased incidence of women and minorities running for office will not affect the voter turnout rates.

COMPARING IDEAS

1. In small groups, compare notes. What information do you have that your classmates don't? What information do they have that you don't?

2. In small groups, compare your answers to the preceding questions. If you have different answers, check your notes and discuss your reasons for making your choices.

3. Compare your rewritten notes to the sample rewritten notes in Appendix C. Notice the organization. Is yours similar or different? Are your notes equally effective in making important ideas stand out?

USING VOCABULARY

You will hear vocabulary from the lecture and discussion in different contexts. Listen before reading each exercise. After listening, circle the letter of the closest paraphrase of the information that you heard.

1. a. He was proposed as a candidate, and he hopes that he can reach his goal.
   b. He was ordered to run for office, but he chose not to do so.
   c. He was recommended as a candidate, but he chose not to be one.

2. a. People were upset because the candidate was expressing ideas that were not in line with the agreed upon ideas of the party.
   b. People were upset because the candidate was expressing negative feelings about the party.
   c. People were upset because the candidate was debating and arguing with too many people in the party.

3. a. She spent more on drinking than anyone else in history.
   b. She spent more to reach her political goal than anyone else in history.
   c. She spent more on her company and its subsidiaries than anyone else in history.

4. a. The athlete was too slow when running in the race; therefore, he stopped running.
   b. The athlete stopped racing because he found that it took too much time from his personal life.
   c. The politician stopped his campaign because campaigning took too much time.

5. a. People buy wood in order to build houses.
   b. People go to special places to vote.
   c. People read public surveys before they vote.

6. a. She was pleased with married life.
   b. She was apathetic about married life.
   c. She was disappointed in married life.

7. a. He feels close to his friends and communicates easily with them.
   b. He feels distant from his friends and feels that there are problems in communication.

8. a. The most important influences on voter turnout are race, ethnicity, and education, in that order.
   b. Education is the most important influence on voter turnout, and this holds true no matter what racial or ethnic group one looks at.
   c. Education is the most important influence on voter turnout for most, but not all, ethnic and racial groups.

RETAINING VOCABULARY

Write ten words from the lecture, article, and discussion that you would like to remember. Use each word in an example that will remind you of its meaning.

Example:

candidate: The presidential candidate made a speech explaining why he would be a better choice than his opponent.

1. _____

_____

2. _____

_____

3. _____

_____

4. _____

_____

5. _____

_____

6. _____

_____

7. _____

_____

8. _____

_____

9. _____

_____

10. _____

_____

WRITING ACTIVITY

The *Los Angeles Times* article on page 145 suggests that the system of voting used in the United States, the "winner takes all" system, has some serious drawbacks. The article mentions other systems and their pros and cons. Based on your experience and knowledge, which of the author's points do you agree with? Which do you disagree with? Write a letter to the editor in response to the article.

PRE-LECTURE DISCUSSION

Vocabulary
Related to Art

sculpture
printmaking

medium:
   watercolor
   oil
   charcoal
   acrylic paint
   pastel

canvas
easel

portrait
landscape
still life
abstract art

photograph/
   photography
in focus
out of focus
focal point
to focus
to develop film

composition
perspective
2-D (two-dimensional)
3-D (three-dimensional)

line:
   diagonal
   horizontal
   vertical
   zigzag

shape:
   square
   rectangle/rectangular
   triangle/triangular
   circle/circular
   oval/ovular

texture
shade
shading

Look at the artwork on this page and pages 150–151. Which ones do you like the best? The least? Rank them from 1 to 6, with 1 being your favorite.

_____ Franz Kline, *Painting Number 2*
_____ Vincent Van Gogh, *Hospital Corridor at Saint-Remy*
_____ Dorothea Lange, *Migrant Mother, Nipomo, California*
_____ Harry Callahan, *Weeds in Snow*
_____ Edgar Degas, *The Orchestra of the Opera*
_____ Edward Hopper, *Early Sunday Morning*

Liking a piece of art does not necessarily mean you would want to have it in your home. Which, if any, of these selections would you like to have in your home? Why? Which would you not like to have in your home? Why not?

Franz Kline (American, 1910–1962), *Painting Number 2*, 1954
Oil on canvas 6'8½" x 8'9" (204.3 x 271.6 cm.)

Vincent Van Gogh (Dutch, 1853–1890), *Hospital Corridor at Saint-Remy*, 1889
Gouache and watercolor on paper, 24⅛" x 18⅝" (61.3 x 47.3 cm.)

Dorothea Lange (American, 1895–1965), *Migrant Mother, Nipomo, California*, 1936.
Gelatin silver print (photograph)

Harry Callahan (American, 1912–1999), *Weeds in Snow*, 1943
Gelatin silver print (photograph)

Edgar Degas (French, 1834–1917), *The Orchestra of the Opera*, 1870
Oil on canvas

Edward Hopper (American, 1882–1967), *Early Sunday Morning*, 1930
Oil on canvas, 35" x 60" (88.9 x 152.4 cm.)

PREPARING FOR THE LECTURE

The title of the lecture is "How to Look at Art." How do you look at art? What do you expect the lecturer to talk about? Brainstorm ideas with your classmates.

LISTENING FOR THE LARGER PICTURE

Read the following questions before the lecture begins. Then, listen to the lecture once without taking notes. While listening, answer the questions.

1. What is "directed looking"?

_____

_____

_____

2. What are the five components (the five categories of observation) of "directed looking"?

a. _____

b. _____

c. _____

d. _____

e. _____

ORGANIZATION

The lecture demonstrates three different organizational plans: *classifying subtopics, exemplifying a topic*, and *describing characteristics*. The lecturer begins by talking about art appreciation in general and then focuses on (and defines) one approach to art appreciation: directed looking. The lecturer then explains "directed looking" by talking about its five components: five categories of observation. Within each category, the lecturer gives examples and descriptions showing how one can apply this type of observation to a given work of art.

DEFINING VOCABULARY

 The following words were used in the lecture that you just heard. You may remember the contexts in which you heard them. You will hear an additional example of each word in a new context. After listening, circle the letter of the definition that most closely matches what you think the word means.

1. appreciation
   a. a sense of need
   b. a sense of disappointment and sadness
   c. a sense of understanding and enjoyment

2. emotion
   a. movement
   b. difficulty
   c. feeling

3. intuitive
   a. able to understand without using logical reasoning
   b. unable to trust and have confidence in people
   c. able to pay for something expensive

4. illusion
   a. something that is not what it seems to be
   b. something that is a true representation of reality
   c. something that costs a lot of money

5. to overlap
   a. to work overtime
   b. to happen at the same time
   c. to rise above; to be higher than

6. apparent
   a. easily seen or understood
   b. having responsibilities typical of a parent
   c. upsetting or disturbing

7. progress
   a. money; earnings
   b. danger; hazard
   c. advancement; forward movement

8. technique
   a. a way of doing some activity
   b. a scientific or mechanical tool
   c. something to write on

9. to imply
   a. to express in an artistic manner
   b. to express directly; to state clearly
   c. to express indirectly; to suggest

10. explicit
    a. unclear and partly expressed
    b. clear and fully expressed
    c. medically important and necessary

NOTE-TAKING PRACTICE

 Listen to the lecture a second time. Take notes using the following format. The comments in the left margin serve to remind you of the organization of the lecture.

Notice that this lecturer has a more participatory style than some other lecturers. Although the lecturer does the majority of speaking, she encourages students to add their ideas. As a note-taker, you need to listen to both the lecturer and the other students. Notice when the lecturer confirms the students' responses and consider whether there is important information to note.

introduction

definition/explanation Directed Looking

classification of components of "directed looking" with examples and descriptions of each

5 categories of observation:

1.

2.

3.

4.

5.

conclusions

Review and revise your notes. Add information that you remember. If helpful, consider rewriting your notes. Make the relationship between ideas clear and make important ideas stand out.

POST-LECTURE READING AND DISCUSSION

Discuss the following in small groups.

1. Return to the artwork that you discussed before hearing the lecture. Using the technique of "directed looking," analyze two works of art. (The lecturer comments about some aspects of each work but does not comment about every aspect of every work. Therefore, your group discussion should include *your* ideas based on "directed looking" as well as the lecturer's ideas.) When you have finished your discussion, present your ideas to the class.

2. Have you ever been to a museum and wondered how a piece of artwork got selected, why it was considered "good"? How do *you* decide if a piece of artwork is "good" or not?

3. Read the following excerpt.

The matter of aesthetic quality is not simple. At any given moment, there may be a consensus among curators, artists, critics, dealers, and collectors that theoretically determines artistic merit, but a look at history also shows that some things greatly admired later were scorned when first introduced, and vice versa.

For those who want to participate actively in debates on what makes a work "good," we need to create some parameters by which to measure artistic success. My own fairly simple guideline is as follows: Art is a human-created expression that makes me think and feel at the same time. The thoughts and emotions it provokes are either new or different from the way I considered them before; they may tap into something I only suspected or maybe did not know that I knew. Most important (and this is how I ultimately decide merit for myself), good art sustains my interest over time, perhaps for its original appeal, perhaps for reasons that are new each time I see it.

What is this writer's criteria for "good" art? Do you agree or disagree with this writer's view? In what ways?

USING YOUR NOTES

Use your notes to answer the following questions.

1. True or False?
   _____ a. A "directed looking" approach to art appreciation requires knowledge about the historical setting of the artwork.
   _____ b. The five categories of observation in a "directed looking" approach to art never overlap.
   _____ c. Abstract paintings never have a subject matter.

2. Name the five categories of observation in a "directed looking" approach and briefly explain them.

   a. _____
   _____

   b. _____
   _____

   c. _____
   _____

   d. _____
   _____

   e. _____
   _____

3. Give four examples of different physical properties of art that one might look at when using a "directed looking" approach to art appreciation.

   a. _____
   b. _____
   c. _____
   d. _____

4. What are two techniques for creating the illusion of distance?

   a. _____
   b. _____

5. Analyze Lange's photograph *Migrant Mother: Nipomo, California* in terms of subject matter, formal elements, and viewer perspective.

   a. subject matter _____
   _____

   b. formal elements _____
   _____

   c. viewer perspective _____
   _____

COMPARING IDEAS

1. In small groups, compare notes. What information do you have that your classmates don't? What information do they have that you don't?

2. In small groups, compare your answers to the preceding questions. If you have different answers, check your notes and discuss your reasons for making your choices.

3. Compare your rewritten notes to the sample rewritten notes in Appendix C. Notice the organization. Is yours similar or different? Are your notes equally effective in making important ideas stand out?

USING VOCABULARY

 You will hear vocabulary from the lecture, reading, and discussion in different contexts. Listen before reading each exercise. After listening, circle the letter of the closest paraphrase of the information that you heard.

Group A

1. a. My friend let me use her new camera.
   b. My friend suggested ways to use my new camera.
   c. My friend gave me some money to buy a new camera.

2. a. My first pictures were very clear.
   b. My first pictures weren't very clear.

3. a. I tried to photograph some people indoors.
   b. I tried to photograph a landscape.
   c. I tried to photograph some arranged objects.

4. a. I wanted to create an illusion of a red rose on a table.
   b. I wanted people to immediately notice the red rose.

Group B

1. a. My boss told me explicitly that he doesn't think I'm working fast enough.
   b. My boss told me indirectly that he doesn't think I'm working fast enough.

2. a. He never shows anger concerning things I do.
   b. He never shows pleasure concerning things I do.
   c. He never shows interest concerning things I do.

3. a. It's a good thing that I enjoy my role as a parent.
   b. It's easy to see that I'm not happy.
   c. I can see that no one around here is happy.

Group C

1. a. She can't always explain her feelings about people, but she is usually right.
   b. She is very logical and always has good reasons for liking or disliking people.

RETAINING VOCABULARY

Write ten words from the lecture and discussion that you would like to remember. Use each word in an example that will remind you of its meaning.

Example:

shade: <u>Some shades of blue look good on me, but other shades don't.</u>

1. _____

   _____

2. _____

   _____

3. _____

   _____

4. _____

   _____

5. _____

   _____

6. _____

   _____

7. _____

   _____

8. _____

   _____

9. _____

   _____

10. _____

   _____

SPEAKING AND LISTENING ACTIVITY

Bring in a copy or slide of a piece of artwork that you like. Give a short presentation about the artwork, talking about the work in terms of the different categories of directed looking.

PRE-LECTURE READING AND DISCUSSION

Vocabulary
Related to Robots,
Computers, and
Medical
Technology

robot
robotics

cyberspace
Internet
the World Wide Web
   (WWW)

to surf the Net
to program a computer
to enter/input data
to save/store information
to log on
to log off

computer screen
computer keyboard
mouse
joystick
computer software
computer hardware
computer chip
computer memory
microprocessor

virtual reality

surgery
surgeon
   neurosurgeon
   orthopedic surgeon
   pediatric surgeon

operating room
operating table

scalpel
incision

imaging tools
   CT (computer
   tomography) scan
   MRI (magnetic reso-
   nance imaging) scan

to remove/excise a
   tumor
to set a bone
to suture/stitch
to transplant
to implant
to anesthetize/anesthesia

Discuss the following in small groups.

1. In the past 100 years, what have been some of the major advances in medical treatment? (Consider drugs, scientific knowledge, technology, etc.)

2. Read the article below. Then discuss your answers to the questions that follow.

Cybersurgery

Computers, Cameras and Robots are Creating an Improved Operating System for Doctors

Jane E. Stevens, *Los Angeles Times*

Colonel Richard Satava has a vision for medicine. He sees it shifting its focus from blood and guts to bits and bytes. Satava, program manager for advanced medical technologies at the Defense Department's Advanced Research Projects Agency, has been a driving force in bringing virtual reality to medicine, where computers create a "virtual" or simulated environment for surgeons and other medical practitioners.

"With virtual reality we'll be able to put a surgeon in every foxhole," said Satava, a U.S. Army surgeon. He envisions a time when soldiers who are wounded fighting overseas are put in mobile surgical units equipped with computers.

The computers would transmit images of the soldiers to surgeons back in the U.S. The surgeons would look at the soldier through virtual reality helmets that contain a small screen displaying the image of the wound and cover the eyes to block out the real world. The doctors would use their hands to guide robotic instruments in the battlefield mobile surgical unit that operate on the soldier.

Although Satava's vision may be years away from standard operating procedure, scientists are progressing toward virtual reality surgery. Engineers at SRI International in Palo Alto [California] are developing a tele-operating device. As surgeons watch a three-dimensional image of the surgery, they move instruments that are connected to a computer, which passes their movements to robotic instruments that perform the surgery. The computer provides feedback to the surgeon on force, textures, and sound.

These technological wonders may not yet be part of the community hospital setting but increasingly some of the machinery is finding its way into civilian medicine. At Wayne State University Medical School, neurosurgeon Lucia Zamorano takes images of the brain from state-of-the-art magnetic resonance (MRI) and computer tomography (CT) scans and uses a computer program to produce a 3-D image. She can then maneuver the 3-D image on the computer screen to map the shortest, least invasive surgical path to the tumor. Zamorano is also using technology that attaches a probe to surgical instruments so that she can track their positions. While excising a tumor deep in the brain, she watches the movement of her surgical tools in a computer graphics image of the patient's brain taken before surgery.

During endoscopic procedures—operations that are done through small incisions in the body in which a miniature camera and surgical tools are maneuvered—surgeons are wearing 3-D glasses for a better view. And they are commanding robot surgeons to cut away tissue more accurately than human surgeons can.

Satava says, "We are in the midst of a fundamental change in the field of medicine."

a. Who is Richard Satava? What is his vision of medical treatment in the future?

b. Find examples in the article of current medical uses for computers, cameras, and robots.

c. The article ends with Satava's quote: "We are in the midst of a fundamental change in the field of medicine." Why is this a *fundamental* change? Considering the past, what other changes in medicine would you classify as equally fundamental—that is, changing the field in the most basic and significant ways?

3. Have you (or has someone you know) had any experiences with medical technology? If so, describe the experiences.

PREPARING FOR THE LECTURE

The title of the lecture is "Paging Robodoc: Robots in Medicine." When you hear the word *robot*, what do you imagine? What do you expect the lecturer to talk about? Brainstorm ideas with your classmates.

LISTENING FOR THE LARGER PICTURE

Read the following questions before the lecture begins. Then, listen to the lecture once without taking notes. After listening, answer the questions.

1. The lecturer's goal is to tell the audience something about robots in medicine. This is a broad topic, so the lecturer only covers some aspects of the topic. Which of the following does the lecturer do? (Check all correct answers.)

_____ a. defines *robot*

_____ b. provides historical background about the use of robots in hospitals

_____ c. explains the essential parts of a robot

_____ d. gives an example of one particular use of robots in hospitals, Robodoc

_____ e. gives numerous examples of robots used in hospitals

_____ f. classifies different types of hospital-based robots

_____ g. describes the process of how Robodoc works

_____ h. speaks about some people's resistance or fears about robots in the operating room

2. To explore the use of robots in the operating room, hip surgery was an obvious choice because it is _____ . (Check all correct answers.)

_____ a. a physically laborious type of surgery

_____ b. performed infrequently

_____ c. performed frequently

_____ d. more accurate when done with robot assistance

_____ e. cheaper when done with robot assistance

ORGANIZATION

The lecture primarily demonstrates three organizational plans: *defining a term, exemplifying a topic,* and *describing a process.* The lecturer begins by defining *robot,* and then gives information about the essential components of robots (the microprocessor, an arm with five or six joints, and the end effector). Then, the lecturer speaks in detail about one example of the use of robots in hospitals: Robodoc, a robot used in hip replacement surgery. The lecturer explains why robots are particularly suited for this type of surgery and describes the process of how it works. At the end, the lecturer concludes by mentioning some expressed concerns about robots in the operating room, but generally emphasizing the potential of robots.

DEFINING VOCABULARY

 The following words and expressions were used in the lecture that you just heard. You may remember the contexts in which you heard them. You will hear an additional example of each word or expression in a new context. After listening, circle the letter of the definition that most closely matches what you think the word or expression means.

1. labor
   a. fear, especially relating to responsibilities
   b. work, especially tiring, physical work
   c. love, especially familial love

2. to manipulate
   a. to win a race easily
   b. to fly a plane or other airborne vehicle
   c. to handle or control skillfully

3. task
   a. a question; something needing an answer
   b. a child of any age
   c. a duty; a piece of work that must be done

4. to alter
   a. to lose weight; to go on a diet
   b. to change; to make different
   c. to throw something useless away

5. precision
   a. education
   b. tension; anxiety
   c. exactness

6. steady
   a. firm; sure in position or movement
   b. dirty; unclean
   c. easily moved or shifted

7. manual
   a. automatic; requiring little human labor or input
   b. happening once a year; yearly
   c. using human rather than mechanical energy

8. to carve
    a. to cut a special shape out of a material such as wood or stone
    b. to remove something (e.g., wood) from its natural environment
    c. to draw or paint a portrait
9. to bore
    a. to fill in
    b. to cut or drill through
    c. to read
10. to lose one's grip
    a. to lose an argument
    b. to lose or loosen a tight hold
    c. to lose sight of
11. cavity
    a. a hill or the raised part of a landscape
    b. sugar or substitute sweeteners
    c. a hole or the empty space inside a mass
12. remote control
    a. referring to the inability to control one's life
    b. referring to the ability to control people
    c. referring to the ability to control something from a distance
13. glimpse
    a. a quick look
    b. a short visit
    c. a movie star's protection

In addition to these words, the lecturer also uses certain terms for various body parts, tools, and materials. Check the meaning of the following terms: *femur*, *mallet*, *chisel*, and *cement*.

NOTE-TAKING PRACTICE

 Listen to the lecture a second time. Take notes using the following format. The comments in the left margin serve to remind you of the organization of the lecture.

introduction	
definition of robot	What is a robot?

essential components of robots	
example of robots	Robots in hospitals: e.g., Robodoc
reasons for use in hip surgery	Why esp. useful for hip surgery?
process	How Robodoc works
conclusions	

Review and revise your notes. Add information that you remember. If helpful, consider rewriting your notes. Make the relationship between ideas clear and make important ideas stand out.

POST-LECTURE READING AND DISCUSSION

Discuss the following in small groups.

1. In the lecture, the speaker notes surgeons' concerns and patients' fears. Do you have any fears about the new technologies in medicine? If so, what are they?

2. Robodoc is not alone. Read the following article from *Discover*, a magazine about science and technology, to learn about another robotic surgeon. When you have finished, discuss your answers to the questions that follow.

Robotic Surgery

Surgeons make big incisions because they need to get their hands in the body. But with tiny robotic hands, their incisions would be smaller—and less traumatic.

Kathy A. Svitil, *Discover*

Since it was developed a decade ago, laparoscopic surgery—in which instruments are inserted through small incisions—has been used by surgeons whenever possible. Patients are less traumatized, require shorter hospital stays, and heal faster than with conventional surgery. Yet despite these benefits, laparoscopy is a challenging procedure. "Surgeons find it hard," says Shankar Sastry, an electrical engineer at the University of California at Berkeley. "It's like operating with chopsticks."

Indeed, laparoscopic instruments are mainly limited to scissors, staplers (to close incisions or attach blood vessels), and graspers (to manipulate tissue). The instruments enter the body through a long tube; a video image from a tiny camera called an endoscope poked through another incision guides the surgeon.

For a relatively simple procedure like gallbladder removal, the tools work well enough. But surgeons can't use the instruments to perform complicated tasks like suturing and knot tying. Because of these limitations, says Sastry, most operations can't be performed endoscopically.

However, now Sastry and his Berkeley colleagues have developed laparoscopic tools—including miniature robotic hands with the dexterity to tie knots. "The reason you have to cut a person open is to get the surgeon's hands in there," he says. "But if you can get little instruments in there that let the surgeons feel as if they are working with their hands in a normal procedure, you don't have to have a big incision."

The Berkeley system consists of a pencil-size joystick (one each for the surgeon's right and left hands), a computer, and right-hand and left-hand end effectors—the robotic instruments that snake into the body to perform the actual surgery. In early models, these resembled three-fingered hands. Now each hydraulically powered end effector consists of a single digit, three to four inches long and less than half an inch wide. It has four joints that rotate, swivel, and swing back and forth and a grasper at the end. The result: a finger that functions like an entire hand.

To operate, a surgeon—who can be in the same room as the patient or at a remote location—uses the joysticks just as he would normal surgical instruments. A computer program translates the surgeon's motions into the movements of the end effectors.

The system also has force feedback, which relays to doctors the response of muscles and other tissues to their actions. The feedback makes the procedure feel more like normal surgery. The research team is also working on tactile sensors that will transmit the feel of tissue to the surgeon's fingertips.

"The overall goal," says Sastry, "is pretty lofty: to not cut a person open unless there is just nothing else to do—for instance, if you have to replace a hip, there is no choice but to go in there and remove the old hip—but in every instance to make sutures and cuts that are as small as possible."

a. What is laparoscopic surgery?

b. What are the advantages of laparoscopic surgery?

c. What are the limitations and challenges of traditional laparoscopic surgery?

d. What system have Sastry and his colleagues developed? What are the components of their system? How does the surgeon operate with it?

USING YOUR NOTES

Use your notes to answer the following questions.

1. According to the Robot Industries Association, what is the definition of the term *robot*?

   _____

   _____

2. True or False?

   _____ a. The word *robot* comes from a Czech word meaning "human-like."

   _____ b. According to the Robot Industries Association definition of a robot, a robot may or may not be reprogrammable.

   _____ c. The end effector of a robot looks exactly like a human hand.

   _____ d. Hip replacement surgery is pretty uncommon.

   _____ e. When hip surgery is done manually, surgeons have to carve a cavity and drill holes in a patient's femur.

   _____ f. Robodoc doesn't actually drill a cavity into the patient's bone; Robodoc just tells the surgeon where to drill.

   _____ g. During Robodoc-assisted hip replacement surgery, the surgeon never actually goes near the patient except to do CT scans.

3. Why have surgeons traditionally needed to use cement to hold the hip implant in place? What has been a disadvantage of the cement?

   _____

   _____

   _____

4. Discuss the benefits of hip replacement surgery done by Robodoc as compared to traditional surgical techniques.

   _____

   _____

   _____

   _____

5. Describe the sequence of steps taken when Robodoc is used for hip replacement surgery.

_____

_____

_____

_____

_____

_____

_____

_____

_____

_____

COMPARING IDEAS

1. In small groups, compare notes. What information do you have that your classmates don't? What information do they have that you don't?

2. In small groups, compare your answers to the preceding questions. If you have different answers, check your notes and discuss your reasons for making your choices.

3. Compare your rewritten notes to the sample rewritten notes in Appendix C. Notice the organization. Is yours similar or different? Are your notes equally effective in making important ideas stand out?

USING VOCABULARY

 You will hear vocabulary from the lecture, reading, and discussion in different contexts. Listen before reading each exercise. After listening, circle the letter of the closest paraphrase of the information that you heard.

Group A

1. a. It is necessary for carpenters to be strong.
   b. It is necessary for carpenters to be exact.

2. a. I know a carpenter who uses power tools for large tasks and hand tools for more detail-oriented tasks.
   b. I know a carpenter who doesn't use power tools at all.

3. a. I spent a long time with him in his workshop, and I was surprised at how much physical work was involved in his work.
   b. I passed by and noticed him in his workshop, and I was surprised at how quiet his workshop was.
   c. I passed by and noticed him in his workshop, and I was surprised at how much physical work was involved in his work.

Group B

1. a. My doctor recommended a brain surgeon to me.
   b. My doctor recommended a bone surgeon to me.
   c. My doctor recommended a heart surgeon to me.
2. a. The specialist told me that my operation would require a very tiny cut.
   b. The specialist told me that my operation would take a very short time.
   c. The specialist told me that I had to make a quick decision about my operation.

Group C

1. a. Mountain climbing requires strength.
   b. Mountain climbing requires a firm grip.
2. a. Most mountain climbers use ropes in case they lose hold of the rock.
   b. Most mountain climbers use ropes so that they can pull themselves up the rock.

Group D

1. a. I have a simple test for you.
   b. I have a simple job for you.
   c. I have a simple question for you.
2. a. Type a letter on the computer exactly as you see it.
   b. Type a letter on the computer, making corrections as you go along.
3. a. When you finish typing, exit the computer system.
   b. When you finish typing, begin another letter.
   c. When you finish typing, call me over.

RETAINING VOCABULARY

Write ten words from the lecture, article, and discussion that you would like to remember. Use each word in an example that will remind you of its meaning.

Example:

incision: The surgeon made an incision that was virtually unnoticeable.

1. _____

_____

2. _____

_____

3. _____

_____

4. _____

_____

5. _____

_____

6. _____

_____

7. _____

_____

8. _____

_____

9. _____

_____

10. _____

_____

WRITING ACTIVITY

Write about one of the following topics.

1. What do you think medical care will be like 100 years from now? Use information from the lecture, articles, and your imagination to describe a hospital or medical center of the future. Consider some of the following questions: What will doctors' jobs be like? What will patient care be like? What will a hospital look like? How will surgical procedures change?

2. Describe an experience that you had with surgery or medical care. How much information did you have prior to undergoing the treatment? Did you have alternative treatments to consider? In retrospect, were your decisions about treatments, hospitals, and doctors the best ones? Since your experience, have there been innovations in the field that would have made your experience easier?

PRE-LECTURE READING AND DISCUSSION

Vocabulary Related to Earthquakes

earthquake
quake
temblor
tremor
aftershock
foreshock

to shake
to vibrate
seismic wave
seismic activity

Richter scale
earthquake magnitude

epicenter
fault (line/zone)
tectonic plate
the Earth's crust

seismologist
seismology

destruction/to destroy
devastation/to devastate
damage/to damage
collapse/to collapse
in ruins

earthquake preparedness

Additional Vocabulary

Discuss the following in small groups.

1. Many people have vivid memories about what they were doing, feeling, and thinking when a major world event occurred (e.g., an earthquake, a volcanic eruption, a tornado, the news report of the death or assassination of an important person). Share your memories with your classmates.

2. Read the following excerpt from a newspaper science column. Then, answer the questions that follow.

Q: What site on Earth has the most earthquakes?

A: According to Craig Brunstein of the United States Geological Survey in Denver, no single site qualifies for the honor. Rather, the highest number of earthquakes occur all around the rim of the Pacific Ocean in the so-called ring of fire, where the movement of tectonic plates is the greatest. That ring includes all of the west coast of North and South America, Japan, the Philippines, Indonesia, New Guinea, and New Zealand. This area has not only the largest number of quakes, but also the most severe ones.

What other information do you already know about earthquakes? What do you know about "tectonic plates"? Brainstorm with your class to share information about the causes and locations of earthquakes. When you listen to the lecture, you can verify your information and learn more.

3. Read the excerpt below. Then, answer the questions that follow.

Warning from Space?

A Russian Scientist Claims He Has Devised a System for Detecting Earthquakes from Outer Space Several Hours before They Hit. U.S. Experts Remain Doubtful

Richard C. Paddock and Robert Lee Hotz, *Los Angeles Times*

Moscow—A Russian scientist says he has come up with a way to predict earthquakes from outer space that could provide a warning as much as three hours in advance of major quakes. The method of forecasting proposed by physics professor Arkady Galper is based on the discovery that electromagnetic waves emanating from Earth just before a big temblor appear to change the behavior of particles in the radiation belt that rings the planet.

Galper, director of the Institute of Space Physics at the Moscow Engineering and Physics Institute, said . . .

According to the article, what does Galper believe he has discovered? What are the reactions of some in the scientific community? Have you heard of any other techniques for earthquake prediction? Share your information with your classmates.

PREPARING FOR THE LECTURE

The title of the lecture is "Earthquakes: Can They Be Predicted?" What do you expect the lecturer to talk about? Brainstorm ideas with your classmates.

LISTENING FOR THE LARGER PICTURE

 Read the following lecture summary and questions. Then, listen to the lecture once without taking notes. Refer to the diagrams on this page as the lecturer talks.

The lecturer defines the term *earthquakes* and then explains the causes of earthquakes. Then, the lecturer explains the process of stress buildup and stress release, partly by comparing the process to familiar objects such as bent wooden sticks or rubber bands. Then, the lecturer describes different types of earthquake prediction techniques that have been investigated—short-range prediction studies and long-range prediction studies. Based on these studies, the lecturer reaches some conclusions about whether earthquakes can be predicted.

Deformation of Rocks	Deformation of a Limber Stick
A. Original position	A. Original position
B. Buildup of strain	B. Buildup of strain
C. Slippage	C. Rupture
D. Strain released	D. Strain released

After listening, work in small groups to answer the following questions.

1. Look at the diagrams again. This time, use your own words to explain what the images demonstrate.
2. What are some examples of short-range earthquake prediction techniques that have been explored or are being explored?
3. What do scientists look at when they search for long-range prediction tools?
4. What conclusions does the lecturer reach about earthquake prediction?

ORGANIZATION

The lecture primarily demonstrates four organizational plans: *describing a causal relationship, describing a process, classifying,* and *making a generalization and providing evidence.* In order to explain the cause of earthquakes, the lecturer describes the process of stress buildup, slippage, and release. In order to make a generalization about the effectiveness of earthquake prediction tools, the lecturer classifies earthquake prediction strategies as either short range or long range, describes studies about them, and looks at their success rates.

DEFINING VOCABULARY

 The following words were used in the lecture that you just heard. You may remember the contexts in which you heard them. You will hear an additional example of each word in a new context. After listening, circle the letter of the definition that most closely matches what you think the word means.

1. remote
   a. polluted; dirty
   b. heavily populated
   c. distant; far

2. rapid
   a. fast
   b. intelligent
   c. careful

3. to radiate
   a. to do physical work outdoors
   b. to do the same work repeatedly
   c. to send out light or heat

4. to deform
   a. to spoil the form or appearance of
   b. to form something repeatedly
   c. to create different forms of music

5. flexible
   a. related to future plans or obligations
   b. able to be bent or changed easily
   c. not able to be bent or changed easily

6. to exceed
   a. to be less than
   b. to be equal to
   c. to be greater than

7. phenomenon
   a. an event that is common and regularly seen
   b. an event that is not common or regularly seen
   c. an event that has never been seen

8. to precede
   a. to forget
   b. to happen later; to go after
   c. to happen earlier; to go before

9. peculiar
    a. dangerous; violent
    b. unusual; strange
    c. friendly; helpful

10. to emit
    a. to send out; to release
    b. to paint
    c. to allow air to enter

11. to foretell
    a. to repeat or tell secret information to others
    b. to have economic problems
    c. to tell what will happen in the future

12. to evacuate
    a. to destroy a building or other structure
    b. to successfully fight a spreading fire
    c. to leave or make people leave a threatened place

13. skeptical
    a. excited; pleased and hopeful
    b. doubting; distrustful; unwilling to believe
    c. trusting; willing to believe

14. cyclical
    a. happening in a regular repeated order
    b. related to technology and scientific research
    c. related to wheeled vehicles (e.g., motorcycles, bicycles)

15. interval
    a. a medical checkup
    b. a break or vacation from work
    c. a period of time between events

16. virtually
    a. luckily; fortunately
    b. all
    c. almost; very nearly

NOTE-TAKING PRACTICE

 Listen to the lecture a second time. Take notes using the following format. The comments in the left margin serve to remind you of the organization of the lecture.

introduction	
definition	Earthquake:
causes	Causes of quakes?

description of plate tectonics and elastic rebound process

research on quake prediction

2 types quake prediction:

short-range prediction:

1st type of prediction strategy

2nd type of prediction strategy

long-range prediction:

conclusions

Review and revise your notes. Add information that you remember. If helpful, consider rewriting your notes. Make the relationship between ideas clear and make important ideas stand out.

POST-LECTURE READING AND DISCUSSION

Read the remainder of the article that you started on page 168. Then, work in small groups to answer the questions that follow.

Warning from Space?

A Russian Scientist Claims He Has Devised a System for Detecting Earthquakes from Outer Space Several Hours before They Hit. U.S. Experts Remain Doubtful

Richard C. Paddock and Robert Lee Hotz, *Los Angeles Times*

Moscow—A Russian scientist says he has come up with a way to predict earthquakes from outer space that could provide a warning as much as three hours in advance of major quakes. The method of forecasting proposed by physics professor Arkady Galper is based on the discovery that electromagnetic waves emanating from Earth just before a big temblor appear to change the behavior of particles in the radiation belt that rings the planet.

Galper, director of the Institute of Space Physics at the Moscow Engineering and Physics Institute, said three groups of Russian scientists have corroborated his results. But no major scientific papers have been published on his earthquake forecasting idea and it has not been subjected to the scrutiny of peer review that is standard in the United States.

Indeed, several U.S. earthquake experts queried about Galper's work were deeply skeptical, saying that there was little evidence to support it or any other prediction theory.

Although many researchers over the years have proposed various techniques to predict earthquakes, none have worked in practice. "Most scientists would say that earthquake prediction is a very long way off, if not impossible," said Thomas Henyey, director of the Southern California Earthquake Center.

Henyey called the Russian prediction theory "implausible." To take it

seriously, Henyey said, "I would have to see a very, very, careful discussion of the physics of the entire process. You have to be skeptical as to whether some theoretical physicist is stringing together phenomena that may seem plausible but that are extremely unlikely to ever happen in nature. You would also want to see that there have been multiple successes, and one would have to look at that very carefully, too."

Galper acknowledged that, so far, his method of prediction is largely theoretical and would require the launch of at least three satellites and the creation of a ground-based network that could rapidly process data from space . . .

Galper said he and his colleagues happened on the possibility of forecasting earthquakes while studying the 600-mile-high radiation belt that encircles the planet's tropical region like a giant doughnut. Early on, they observed an occasional unexpected "bulge" in the belt as particles dipped down—or "fell out"—in the direction of Earth for periods of 10 to 15 minutes. Although sampling of the radiation belt was normally limited to two hours a week, they happened one day in 1985 to record a large amount of "falling out" activity. The same period, they noticed, had been one of high seismic activity on Earth, and they speculated that there could be a connection. In 1989, a seismic measuring station in the San Francisco Bay area near the

site of the Loma Prieta [California] earthquake found that electromagnetic waves emanated from the epicenter three hours before the temblor struck. Theorizing that such radiation could affect particle movement in near space, they analyzed the timing of the bulges they had discovered. Galper said that in about 80 out of about 100 cases analyzed, his research team has found a correlation between the unusual behavior of the space particles and the electromagnetic radiation transmitted before major earthquakes.

Because of a time lag of several days in retrieving the data from space, the scientists have never predicted a quake. "Our system is not designed for rapid feeding of information," Galper said . . .

To establish an earthquake warning system for the entire planet would require a large network of satellites. But Galper said it would be possible to cover the region where 90% of quakes occur—and where most of the world's population lives—with three satellites.

When a satellite detected a bulge in the belt, the information would immediately be routed to a communications satellite that would feed the information to stations on the ground. There, the data would be rapidly processed to estimate the location of the epicenter within an area of 60 square miles. The affected region would be notified and the public would have as much as three hours to prepare for the quake.

1. Several earthquake experts are doubtful about Galper's work. Give at least four reasons for their skepticism.

2. Galper's claims are purely "theoretical" right now. What does this mean?

3. Describe Galper's idea for creating an earthquake warning system.

4. According to the article, are Galper's ideas impossible?

USING YOUR NOTES

Use your notes to answer the following questions.

1. An earthquake is the v_____ of the Earth produced by the rapid release of e_____ .

2. Name five different kinds of short-range prediction strategies that researchers have examined.

   a. _____

   b. _____

   c. _____

   d. _____

   e. _____

3. True or False?

   _____ a. Most earthquakes are caused by volcanic eruptions.

   _____ b. Chinese seismologists successfully forecast a large earthquake and saved thousands of lives.

   _____ c. Since 1975, Chinese seismologists have repeatedly been able to predict serious earthquakes.

   _____ d. Researchers who try to make long-range predictions focus on finding historical cycles or patterns.

   _____ e. Seismologists found one site in California that has had a serious earthquake every twenty-two years, without exception.

   _____ f. According to the lecturer, almost all seismologists believe that short-term earthquake prediction is difficult, if not impossible.

   _____ g. There are more scientists who believe that short-range prediction tools will be found than scientists who believe that long-range prediction tools will be found.

4. In a paragraph, explain how a flexible stick, a rubber band, and a stone thrown in a pond can demonstrate aspects of the earthquake process.

   _____

   _____

   _____

   _____

   _____

   _____

   _____

   _____

   _____

COMPARING IDEAS

1. In small groups, compare notes. What information do you have that your classmates don't? What information do they have that you don't?

2. In small groups, compare your answers to the preceding questions. If you have different answers, check your notes and discuss your reasons for making your choices.

3. Compare your rewritten notes to the sample rewritten notes in Appendix C. Notice the organization. Is yours similar or different? Are your notes equally effective in making important ideas stand out?

USING VOCABULARY

 You will hear vocabulary from the lecture, discussion, and reading in different contexts. Listen before reading each exercise. After listening, circle the letter of the closest paraphrase of the information that you heard.

Group A

1. a. The train goes by at 1:20, 2:20, 3:20, etc.
   b. The train will go by in twenty minutes.
   c. The train goes by every twenty minutes.

2. a. You can always hear a whistle while it is passing.
   b. You can always hear a whistle before it passes.
   c. You can always hear a whistle after it passes.

3. a. It goes by slowly and never goes close to the speed limit.
   b. It goes by too fast, beyond the speed limit.
   c. It goes by fast, but not beyond the speed limit.

4. a. Occasionally, I notice that the dishes and other objects crack when it passes.
   b. Occasionally, I notice that the dishes and other objects shake when it passes.
   c. Occasionally, I notice that the dishes and other objects get dirty when it passes.

Group B

1. a. The general wanted the people in the village to leave before the enemy got there.
   b. The general wanted the people in the village to stay and fight in order to protect the village from the enemy.

2. a. The problem is that the village is far and has fewer than 1,000 people.
   b. The problem is that the village is poor and the 1,000 residents are peculiar.
   c. The problem is that the village is far and has more than 1,000 people.

3. a. The people are frightened because of their previous bad experiences with the general.
   b. The people are questioning the truth of the general's words because of previous bad experiences with him.
   c. The people are angry because of their previous bad experiences with the general.

4. a. No one can speak to the villagers.
   b. No one knows what the future will be for the villagers.
   c. No one knows anyone personally in the village.

RETAINING VOCABULARY

Write ten words from the lecture, article, and discussion that you would like to remember. Use each word in an example.

Example:

collapse: <u>The building collapsed during the earthquake, and no one has rebuilt it.</u>

1. _____

_____

2. _____

_____

3. _____

_____

4. _____

_____

5. _____

_____

6. _____

_____

7. _____

_____

8. _____

_____

9. _____

_____

10. _____

_____

SPEAKING AND LISTENING ACTIVITY

Read an article from the library or the Internet related to earthquakes (e.g., earthquake prediction, earthquake historical data, country- or region-specific earthquake information, earthquake measurement, earthquake preparedness, earthquake engineering). Prepare a five-minute presentation. Explain the main ideas of the article and conclude with your opinion and/or evaluation of these ideas.

17 HALL'S CLASSIFICATION OF CULTURES

PRE-LECTURE DISCUSSION

This lecture is about some of the views of Dr. Edward Hall, an anthropologist who has specialized in how cultures relate to one another. Some of his work has focused on the different assumptions that people have regarding such basic belief systems as attitudes toward time, space, and other people. The following activities are suggested as ways to judge our own attitudes and the attitudes of our friends and our classmates about these subjects.

1. The Personal Space Test

How much distance do you require between you and a conversational partner? Have you ever been in a conversation with someone and felt that the other person was standing too close to you? Have you ever been in the opposite situation, in which the person that you were talking to seemed to be inching away from you? These are issues involving the amount of personal space with which you feel comfortable. The Personal Space Test allows you to compare your sphere of personal space with those of your classmates.

> Two people have a conversation during which Person A continues to move gradually closer to Person B, while Person B remains standing in the same spot. Person A continues to move closer until Person B says that he or she is uncomfortable with the closeness. The conversation should begin with the participants approximately three feet apart, and Person A should move closer at increments of approximately three inches. Measure the distance between Persons A and B when Person B says that he or she is uncomfortable. The experiment should then be repeated, with Person A and Person B switching roles.

Discuss with the class how you felt during this experiment. How did you feel when your conversation partner was too close? Too far? Did you notice differences between how people judged what was too close or too far? Do you think that culture has anything to do with people's expectations of personal space? Try this experiment with pairs from the same culture. Do they tend to agree about their comfort zones?

2. Attitudes toward Time

Circle the number that corresponds to your feelings about each statement. Use the following scale.
1 disagree strongly
2 disagree somewhat
3 neither agree nor disagree
4 agree somewhat
5 agree strongly

a. I get impatient when someone is late.	1	2	3	4	5
b. I am rarely late.	1	2	3	4	5

    c. I would be insulted if someone was supposed to
        meet me at 10:00 and arrived at 10:15 and didn't
        apologize or give me a good excuse.   1 2 3 4 5
    d. If I have a party and invite people for 7:00, I expect
        them to really show up at 7:00, not 7:30.   1 2 3 4 5
    e. I believe the expression "Time is money" has some
        truth to it.   1 2 3 4 5
    f. I get upset when I feel as if I'm wasting time.   1 2 3 4 5
    g. I always wear a wristwatch.   1 2 3 4 5
    h. I try to do as much as possible in one day and I get
        frustrated if something (e.g., traffic) prevents me
        from doing what I want.   1 2 3 4 5

Calculate your score. What does your score tell you about your attitude toward time? Are there any great variations in scores in the class? Do you think any of the variations are due to cultural attitudes? Try giving this questionnaire to people from different cultures and see if the scores change.

3. Attitudes toward Interpersonal Relationships

Circle the number that corresponds to your feelings about each statement. Use the following scale.

    1 disagree strongly
    2 disagree somewhat
    3 neither agree nor disagree
    4 agree somewhat
    5 agree strongly

    a. If I enter into a verbal contract with someone, I
        always keep my word.   1 2 3 4 5
    b. If someone enters into a verbal contract with me,
        I trust them and do not feel it is necessary to get it
        all on paper.   1 2 3 4 5
    c. I would not marry a person who came from a
        disreputable family.   1 2 3 4 5
    d. I would never do something that would shame my
        family, even if I believed it was right.   1 2 3 4 5
    e. If there is corruption in a company, I believe that
        the head of that company should take responsibility,
        even if she or he was not involved.   1 2 3 4 5
    f. In decisions involving what is best for me as an
        individual versus what is best for my family as a
        whole, I will always decide on the side of my family.   1 2 3 4 5

Calculate your score. What does your score tell you about your attitude toward interpersonal relationships? Are there any great variations in scores in the class? Are any of the variations due to cultural attitudes? Try giving this questionnaire to people from different cultures and see if the scores change.

4. Discussion

What do the following two statements mean? Do you agree or disagree? Why?

    a. All human beings are captives of their culture.
    b. What we think of as mind is really internalized culture.

PREPARING FOR THE LECTURE

The title of the lecture is "Hall's Classification of Cultures." What do you expect the lecturer to talk about? Brainstorm ideas with your classmates.

LISTENING FOR THE LARGER PICTURE

1. Read the following summary. Then, listen to the lecture once without taking notes. While listening, fill in the blanks.

   The goal of this lecture is to make the audience aware of Hall's classification of cultures on a continuum from _____ to _____ . In order to understand this classification, the lecturer defines certain terms and gives examples of how each type of culture would react in situations involving _____ , _____ , and _____ .

2. Based on your first listening, discuss your answers to the following questions.

   a. In your own words, explain the terms *high-context culture* and *low-context culture*.
   b. Explain how time is viewed by people from high-context and low-context cultures.
   c. Explain how personal space is viewed by people from high-context and low-context cultures.
   d. Explain how interpersonal relationships are viewed by people from high-context and low-context cultures.
   e. Reread the statements about time and interpersonal relationships on pages 177–178. How do you think a person from a high-context culture would respond to them? A person from a low-context culture?

ORGANIZATION

In order to present this *classification* of cultures, the lecturer *defines* each type of culture and gives *examples* of how it functions in real life. These examples are further *classified* in terms of time, space, and personal relationships. The lecture organization can be outlined as follows:

   Introduction

   I. High-context cultures

   A. Definition
   B. Examples regarding interpersonal relationships
   C. Examples regarding attitudes toward time
   D. Examples regarding attitudes toward personal space

   II. Low-context cultures

   A. Definition
   B. Examples regarding interpersonal relationships
   C. Examples regarding attitudes toward time
   D. Examples regarding attitudes toward personal space

   Conclusion

This lecture can also be thought of as demonstrating a *comparison and contrast* pattern, because the two items are defined and discussed in order to differentiate them from each other.

DEFINING VOCABULARY

The following words and expressions were used in the lecture that you just heard. You may remember the contexts in which you heard them. You will hear an additional example of each word or expression in a new context. After listening, circle the letter of the definition that most closely matches what you think the word or expression means.

1. ingrained
   a. correct; truthful
   b. firmly established
   c. forced by someone else

2. assumption
   a. a lie that is told in order to deceive another person
   b. a mistake that is made on purpose
   c. a conclusion that is reached without proof or demonstration

3. unconscious
   a. on purpose; intentional
   b. annoying; irritating
   c. without awareness

4. striking
   a. very slight
   b. very noticeable
   c. unimportant

5. continuum
   a. an extreme position; an opposing position
   b. a system of classification based on physical differences
   c. a range between two endpoints

6. entity
   a. an event that takes place indoors
   b. something that exists as a particular and separate unit
   c. an event that takes place outdoors, in natural surroundings

7. negotiation
   a. a demand presented in order to get what one wants
   b. a discussion that occurs in order to reach an agreement
   c. a workers' organization

8. commodity
   a. something useful that can be traded, sold, or saved
   b. something immaterial; something that is not concrete
   c. a group of individuals who interact with each other

9. network
   a. an individual characteristic or quality
   b. a means of transportation
   c. a series of connections and contacts

10. to restrain
    a. to try too hard
    b. to control; to limit behavior
    c. to give someone a prison sentence

11. to feel violated
    a. to feel that one's rights and wishes have been ignored
    b. to feel angry and want to harm others
    c. to feel close to another person and want to help him or her

12. reform
    a. a harsher, more severe punishment
    b. the destruction or elimination of a building
    c. a correction of an injustice

13. rigid
    a. inflexible; not easily changed
    b. flexible; easily changed
    c. extremely cold; below freezing

DEFINING IDIOMS AND SAYINGS

The following idioms and sayings reflect attitudes toward time, space, and interpersonal relationships. You will hear these words in context. After listening, circle the letter of the definition that you think most closely explains the idiom or saying.

1. to shoulder the blame
   a. to blame another person for an action
   b. to take responsibility for an action
   c. to shift responsibility for an action to another person

2. Her word is her bond.
   a. She lies a lot.
   b. She does what she promises.
   c. She talks a lot.

3. to pass the buck
   a. to send money to another person
   b. to shift responsibility to another person
   c. to accept responsibility

4. The buck stops here.
   a. I will take your money.
   b. I will accept responsibility.
   c. I will shift responsibility to someone else.

5. Time is money.
   a. Time can be viewed in terms of money lost, earned, or wasted.
   b. Money can help you live longer (e.g., buy better medical care).
   c. Money can buy happy times (e.g., parties).

NOTE-TAKING PRACTICE

Listen to the lecture a second time. Take notes using the following format. The comments in the left margin serve to remind you of the organization of the lecture.

introduction	
cultures: type 1	High-context cultures
definition	
examples re: interpersonal relationships	
examples re: personal space	
examples re: time	
disadvantages	
advantages	
cultures: type 2	Low-context cultures
definition	
examples re: interpersonal relationships	
examples re: personal space	
examples re: time	
disadvantages	

advantages

Low-context		High-context
German-Swiss German Scandinavian U.S. French English Italian Spanish Greek Arab		

conclusions

Review and revise your notes. Add information that you remember. If helpful, consider rewriting your notes. Make the relationship between ideas clear and make important ideas stand out.

POST-LECTURE READING AND DISCUSSION

Discuss the following in small groups.

1. Read and imagine the following international business scenario described by an Indian business executive, Kurien Joseph.

> I remember visiting the newly independent nation of Turkmenistan in 1992. At the first meeting, in Askhabad, I was received by a team of six or seven executives at 10 A.M. My next appointment was at 11:30 A.M.
>
> This meeting started off with a long speech, with intermittent translations by my interpreter about how wonderful they felt to receive me, an Indian, from the country of Babar, Humayun,[1] and so on. After more than ten minutes of these obviously heart-felt sentiments, I got a chance to respond.
>
> In about a minute or so I reciprocated their sentiments and then, in typical business style, introduced my company, my product range, the advantages of doing business with us, and so on. I finished my spiel in about ten minutes.
>
> Then it was their turn again. This time, each of the remaining five or six executives spoke. As I learned later, each of them was the head of a particular department and therefore had something specific to discuss. I had my notebook open and pen at the ready, to pick up any business possibilities. To my utter surprise, and even irritation at that time, each of these executives went into a long speech, welcoming me and speaking about Timur,[2] Samarkand,[3] Babar. It went on till 11:20 A.M.
>
> And then, mercifully, the speeches stopped. I was cordially and quite ceremoniously invited for dinner that evening. "What about our business discussions?" I whispered to my interpreter, in great disappointment. "Oh, that will be tomorrow," he whispered back.

---

[1] **Babar** (1483–1530) founded the Mughal Empire of India. His son, **Humayun**, was the second Mughal Emperor.

[2] **Timur** (1336–1405) conquered lands throughout Asia, including India and Turkmenistan.

[3] **Samarkand**, one of the oldest existing cities in the world, is in Uzbekistan and was the capital of Timur's empire.

a. Apply Hall's theories to the above scenario. How might culturally different expectations explain the different actions and perspectives of the executives from Turkmenistan and India?

b. The Indian business executive also worked in Australia for four years. Would you consider his behavior and attitudes to be closer to the low-context or the high-context end of the continuum? What about the business executives from Turkmenistan?

2. How does Hall's classification system fit when you apply it to your own culture or what you know of other cultures? If your culture was not on the continuum, where would you place it?

3. Do you think that Hall's classification system is valid? Do you see any problems with it? If so, what are they?

4. The lecturer mentions a number of idioms and sayings related to time, space, and interpersonal relationships that are common in American English. Are you familiar with any other idioms or sayings about these themes (in English or another language)? If so, what are they and what do they mean?

USING YOUR NOTES

Use your notes to answer the following questions.

1. How does Hall define the following terms?

a. high-context culture _____

_____

b. low-context culture _____

_____

2. True or False?

_____ a. Edward Hall believes that cultures are either high-context or low-context.

_____ b. Edward Hall believes that most people are aware of their culture's assumptions about time, space, and interpersonal relations.

_____ c. A culture in which who you know is more important than what you know would be a low-context culture.

_____ d. "Business negotiations took place and the participants simply shook hands to finalize the deal." This would be reasonable in a low-context culture.

_____ e. Hall would predict that, generally, members of low-context cultures would not break the law due to the fact that they would not want to bring disgrace to their families.

_____ f. A culture that values individuality would be a high-context culture.

_____ g. Hall would predict that people in low-context cultures would prefer that visitors call before dropping by to visit.

3. What is the difference between a "polychronic" and a "monochronic" view of time? Define each view and give one example of how this view could affect one's acts and attitudes in everyday life.

   a. polychronic view of time _____

   _____

   _____

   b. monochronic view of time _____

   _____

   _____

4. According to Hall, what are the advantages and disadvantages of a high-context culture and a low-context culture?

   a. high-context culture _____

   _____

   _____

   b. low-context culture _____

   _____

   _____

5. Give four examples of how Hall's ideas could have relevance for international business negotiations.

   a. _____

   _____

   b. _____

   _____

   c. _____

   _____

   d. _____

   _____

COMPARING IDEAS

1. In small groups, compare notes. What information do you have that your classmates don't? What information do they have that you don't?
2. In small groups, compare your answers to the preceding questions. If you have different answers, check your notes and discuss your reasons for making your choices.
3. Compare your rewritten notes to the sample rewritten notes in Appendix C. Notice the organization. Is yours similar or different? Are your notes equally effective in making important ideas stand out?

USING VOCABULARY

 You will hear vocabulary from this lecture in different contexts. Listen before reading each exercise. After listening, circle the letter of the closest paraphrase of the information that you heard.

1. a. He won't accept responsibility when things go wrong.
   b. He accepts responsibility when things go wrong.
   c. He refuses to do extra work.

2. a. No one likes to work with her because she steals money.
   b. No one likes to work with her because she never accepts responsibility for her actions.
   c. No one likes to work with her because she always wants credit for the work that other people do.

3. a. There are minor, barely noticeable, differences in the way they negotiate.
   b. There are very noticeable differences in the way they negotiate.
   c. If the negotiations aren't successful, the workers will go on strike.

4. a. The audience was aggressive and loud.
   b. The audience was neither aggressive nor loud.
   c. The audience was loud but not aggressive.

5. a. She tried to steal her neighbor's purse.
   b. She picked up her neighbor's purse without being aware of doing it.
   c. She picked up her neighbor's purse because she wanted to be helpful.

6. a. People have flexible expectations about sex roles, and they can easily change these expectations because they were learned later in life.
   b. People have inflexible and deeply felt expectations about sex roles because they were learned early in life.
   c. People have deeply felt expectations about sex roles. However, these feelings can change.

7. a. She doesn't like privacy and loves it when people visit without calling first.
   b. She feels that her privacy is not respected when people visit without calling first.
   c. She has been physically hurt by visitors who arrived unexpectedly.

8. a. The voters wanted changes in the education system.
   b. The voters wanted a completely new education system.
   c. The voters wanted the leaders to create an education system.

9. a. Knowledge and information refer to the same thing.
   b. Knowledge and information refer to two different things.

10. a. The researcher rated the participants either "happy" or "sad."
    b. The researcher rated the participants "happy," "sad," or somewhere in between.

RETAINING VOCABULARY

Write ten words from the lecture and discussion that you would like to remember. Use each word in an example that will remind you of its meaning.

Example:

assumption: They looked so much alike that I assumed that they were father and son. However, my assumption was incorrect.

1. _____

   _____

2. _____

   _____

3. _____

   _____

4. _____

   _____

5. _____

   _____

6. _____

   _____

7. _____

   _____

8. _____

   _____

9. _____

   _____

10. _____

   _____

WRITING ACTIVITY

Hall's work focuses on cross-cultural differences relating to time, space, and interpersonal relationships. Write about a specific event from your cross-cultural experience that relates to one or more of these categories.

7

POST-COURSEWORK EVALUATION

◐ Goals

- Synthesize note-taking skills learned in previous units
- Evaluate listening comprehension, note-taking skills, and inferencing skills through quizzes consisting of True/False, multiple-choice, and short-answer questions
- Evaluate application of listening comprehension and note-taking skills through extended written responses incorporating lecture information

LECTURE **18** THE PYRAMIDS OF EGYPT: AN ENGINEERING FEAT

PRE-LECTURE READING AND DISCUSSION

Discuss your answers to the following in small groups.

1. What monuments are pictured on page 189? What do you know about their construction and purpose?
2. Read the following article about a recent archaeological find in Egypt. Then, answer the questions that follow.

  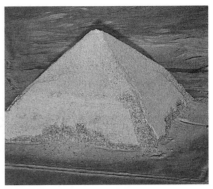

site
foundation

to survey
to level
to plot
to lever
to hoist

mortar
concrete
cement

crane
bulldozer

plywood
lumber
girder
brick

level
ramp
lever

mason/stonemason/
*   masonry*
bricklayer
carpenter/carpentry
surveyor
architect/architecture

blueprint
architectural plan

Additional
Vocabulary

World's Oldest Paved Road Found in Egypt

Thomas H. Maugh II, *Los Angeles Times*

American researchers have discovered the world's oldest paved road, a 4,600-year-old highway that linked a quarry in a desolate region of the Egyptian desert to waterways that carried blocks to monument sites along the Nile.

The eight-mile road is at least 500 years older than any previously discovered road and is the only paved road discovered in ancient Egypt, said geologist Thomas Bown of the United States Geological Survey in Denver, who reported the discovery Friday.

"The road probably doesn't rank with the pyramids as a construction feat, but it is a major engineering achievement," said his colleague, geologist James Harrell of the University of Toledo. "Not only is the road earlier than we thought possible, we didn't even think they built roads."

The researchers made an additional discovery in the quarry at the northern end of the road: the first evidence that the Egyptians used rock saws. "This is the oldest example of saws being used for cutting stone," said archaeologist James K. Hoffmeier of Wheaton College in Illinois.

"That's two technologies we didn't know they had," Harrell said. "And we don't know why they were both abandoned."

The road was discovered in the Faiyum Depression about 45 miles southwest of Cairo. Short segments of the road had been observed by earlier explorers, Bown said, but they failed to realize its significance or follow up on their observations. Bown and his colleagues stumbled across it while they were doing geological mapping in the region.

The road was clearly built to service the newly discovered quarry. Bown and Harrell have found the camp that housed workers at the quarry, and numerous potsherds and artifacts date the site to the Egyptian Old Kingdom that began about 2600 B.C.

The road appears today to go nowhere, ending in the middle of the desert. When it was built, its terminus was a quay on the shore of Lake Moeris, which had an elevation of about 66 feet above sea level, the same as the quay. Birket Qarun, the lake that is now at the bottom of the depression, has a surface elevation of 148 feet below sea level, reflecting the sharp change in climate in the region.

Lake Moeris received its water from the annual floods of the Nile. At the time of the floods, the river and lake were at the same level and connected through a gap in the hills near the modern villages of el-Lahun and Hawara. Harrell and Bown believe that blocks were loaded onto barges during the dry season, then floated over to the Nile during the floods to be shipped off to the monument sites at Giza and Saqqara.

a. What discoveries are mentioned in the article?
b. "The road appears today to go nowhere." Did it really go nowhere? What was the road used for?
c. Why is the discovery important?

PREPARING FOR THE LECTURE

The title of the lecture is "The Pyramids of Egypt: An Engineering Feat." What do you expect the lecturer to talk about? Brainstorm ideas with your classmates.

LISTENING FOR THE LARGER PICTURE

 Read the following questions. Then, listen to the lecture once without taking notes. After listening, answer the questions.

1. Which of the following does the lecturer do?
   _____ a. speaks about the daily life of the ancient Egyptians
   _____ b. speaks about the lives and accomplishments of different ancient Egyptian kings
   _____ c. provides information about when the Egyptian pyramids were constructed
   _____ d. compares and contrasts pyramids built in Egypt to those built in Mexico
   _____ e. gives details to describe one pyramid in particular, the Great Pyramid of Khufu in Giza
   _____ f. describes the three types of pyramids found in Egypt
   _____ g. explains the process required to build the pyramid

2. Why were the Egyptian pyramids built?

   _____

   _____

   _____

DEFINING VOCABULARY

The following words and expressions were used in the lecture that you just heard. You may remember the contexts in which you heard them. You will hear an additional example of each word or expression in a new context. After listening, circle the letter of the definition that most closely matches what you think the word or expression means.

1. feat
   a. a part of the body
   b. an achievement; an act of skill, strength, or imagination
   c. a failure of skill, strength, or imagination

2. tomb
   a. a cemetery
   b. a chamber for the burial of the dead; a monument commemorating the dead
   c. a soldier who died in battle

3. spirit
    a. soul; the central quality or force within someone
    b. body; the physical nature of an individual
    c. death; the loss of life

4. to preserve
    a. to move forward into the future; to progress
    b. to argue because of differences in beliefs or traditions
    c. to protect and stop from changing

5. stable
    a. a piece of furniture with a flat surface on top
    b. not easily upset, changed, or moved; firm
    c. easily upset, changed, or moved; flexible

6. steep slope
    a. a nearly flat surface, changing only slightly in height or angle
    b. a means of transportation (like a bicycle) for climbing hills
    c. a surface set at a large angle, either rising or falling

7. huge
    a. very pretty
    b. very cheap
    c. very big

8. to swell
    a. to increase in roundness and fullness
    b. to treat an injury with an ice pack or heating pad
    c. to fall

9. to drag
    a. to lift above the head in order to carry
    b. to request assistance in order to move something
    c. to cause to move along the ground

10. coffin
    a. a box in which a dead person is buried
    b. a white sheet in which a dead person is buried
    c. a cemetery with separate sections for people of different religions

11. ramp
    a. a type of wheelchair used by people with disabilities
    b. stairs connecting one level to another
    c. a man-made gradual path connecting two different levels

12. to speculate
    a. to think about something without having enough facts to reach a certain conclusion
    b. to take sides in divorce proceedings
    c. to be certain about something

13. to ponder
    a. to swim in order to get exercise
    b. to give advice or suggestions about something
    c. to think deeply about something

In addition to these words, the lecturer also uses terms for various hand tools and construction devices and equipment: wedges, chisels, mallets, ropes, sledges, wheeled vehicles, levers, cranes, bulldozers. The lecturer also refers to a specific stone (limestone) and certain metals (gold, copper, iron, bronze).

NOTE-TAKING PRACTICE AND QUIZ

 Listen to the lecture a second time and take notes. When you finish, review and revise your notes. Add information that you remember. If helpful, consider rewriting your notes. Make the relationship between ideas clear and make important ideas stand out.

In about a week, your teacher will return your notes and give you a quiz on the information in the lecture. The purpose of this activity is to find out how well your notes help you to retain information.

POST-LECTURE DISCUSSION

Discuss your answers to the following questions in small groups.

1. The lecturer ends the lecture by saying:

   > these pyramids of ancient Egypt allow us glimpses into worlds of long ago
   > . . . it makes me wonder when I think about them . . . what is our legacy
   > to the future? . . . what legacy are we going to pass down to our descen-
   > dants? . . . what's going to remain of us and our technological achieve-
   > ments five thousand years in the future? . . . I think these are questions
   > that are worth pondering.

   How would you answer these questions?

2. Imagine that you have been given the job of burying a time capsule for the current year. Everything will be placed in a room-sized box, which is designed to last and protect its contents for 5,000 years. What will you include in that box to give your descendants an accurate idea of life today?

WRITING ACTIVITY

Write an essay on one of the following topics.

1. In what ways does the significance of the pyramids extend beyond their function as burial places for kings? Use data, facts, and information from the lecture to support your ideas. Consider knowledge that we have gained about the religion, social structure, and technology of ancient Egypt. Consider, too, how this knowledge and the ruins of the pyramids might be important to our lives now.

2. a. Discuss what the pyramids tell us about life in Egypt 5,000 years ago. Use data, facts, and information from the lecture to support your ideas.
   b. What modern technological achievements do you think will be remembered 5,000 years from now? What do you think they will show others about our society?

3. a. Discuss how the culture and environment of ancient Egypt impacted the construction and design of the pyramids. Use data, facts, and information from the lecture to support your ideas.
   b. Choose a location that you know well. Discuss how the culture and environment of that location have impacted the design and construction of its buildings (e.g., houses, shopping malls, churches and temples, office buildings).

19 PERFECTIONISM

PRE-LECTURE DISCUSSION

Vocabulary Related to Achieving

to excel
to outdo
to surpass

superiority
inferiority

to live up to (someone's)
    expectations
to meet (someone's)
    expectations

to have standards
    beyond reach
to push oneself

self-worth
self-esteem
self-doubt
self-respect

self-defeating behavior

first-rate
second-rate

to be driven (to do
    something)

Additional Vocabulary

Are you a perfectionist? Take this test and see.

The Perfectionism Scale

If you're not sure whether or not you are a perfectionist, you might want to test yourself with Burns's scale. His inventory lists attitudes or beliefs that people sometimes hold. Use the scale below to indicate how much you agree with each statement:

> +2 agree strongly
> +1 agree
> 0 neutral
> -1 disagree
> -2 disagree strongly

Fill in the blank preceding each statement with the number that best describes how you think most of the time. There are no right or wrong answers, so try to respond according to the way you usually feel and behave.

____ a. If I don't set the highest standards for myself, I am likely to end up a second-rate person.
____ b. People will probably think less of me if I make a mistake.
____ c. If I cannot do something really well, there is little point in doing it at all.
____ d. I should be upset if I make a mistake.
____ e. If I try hard enough, I should be able to excel at anything I attempt.
____ f. It is shameful for me to display weaknesses or foolish behavior.
____ g. I shouldn't have to repeat the same mistake many times.
____ h. An average performance is bound to be unsatisfying to me.
____ i. Failing at something important means I'm less of a person.
____ j. If I scold myself for failing to live up to my expectations, it will help me to do better in the future.

SCORING: Add up your score on all items, noting that plus numbers and minus numbers cancel each other out. For example, if your answer on five items was +1 and your score on the other five was -1, your total test score would be 0. If you answered +2 on all the items, your total score would be +20, revealing a very high degree of perfectionism. If you answered -2 on every item, your score would be -20, signifying a strongly nonperfectionistic mind-set. Preliminary studies suggest that about half of the [American] population is likely to score from +2 to +16, indicating varying degrees of perfectionism.

Share your results with your classmates.

Divide the class into two groups: those who scored on the higher end of the perfectionist scale and those who scored on the lower end. In the groups, discuss the following questions.

1. Do you think you are in the right group? Why or why not?
2. Using your own words, define *perfectionism*.
3. Do you think that your degree of perfectionism helps or hinders your success? Why?

Compare each group's ideas.

PREPARING FOR THE LECTURE

This lecture is about the costs and benefits of perfectionistic attitudes. Before listening to the lecture, write your ideas about each question in the column marked "My Ideas." Discuss your answers with your classmates.

	My Ideas	The Lecturer's Ideas
1. Is a perfectionist attitude a positive or negative trait?		
2. What is "perfectionism"?		
3. Do you think it would be an asset or a hindrance to have a perfectionist attitude in the business world? Why?		
4. Do you think it would be an asset or a hindrance to have a perfectionist attitude in the athletic world? Why?		
5. Do you think it would be an asset or a hindrance to have a perfectionist attitude in the world of education? Why?		
6. Are there emotional costs of perfectionist attitudes? If so, what are they?		

	My Ideas	The Lecturer's Ideas
7. Are there physical costs of perfectionist attitudes? If so, what are they?		
8. Where do perfectionist attitudes come from?		

LISTENING FOR THE LARGER PICTURE

 Listen to the lecture once without taking notes. While listening, try to answer the questions in the preceding section from the lecturer's point of view. After listening, discuss how the lecturer's ideas compare with your own.

DEFINING VOCABULARY

The following words, expressions, and idioms were used in the lecture that you just heard. You may remember the contexts in which you heard them. You will hear an additional example of each word, expression, or idiom in a new context. After listening, write a definition for each word, expression, or idiom.

1. maxim _____

2. no pain, no gain _____

3. pursuit of excellence _____

4. to strain compulsively _____

5. to be prone (to something) _____

6. turmoil _____

7. to be plagued by self-doubt _____

8. to anticipate (something) _____

9. defensive _____

10. to frustrate _____

11. to alienate (someone) _____

12. inevitable _____

13. cream of the crop _____

14. dichotomy _____

15. to reach the point of diminishing returns _____

16. to distort _____

17. impaired _____

18. to be preoccupied with deadlines _____

19. incidence _____

20. trait _____

NOTE-TAKING PRACTICE AND QUIZ

 Listen to the lecture a second time and take notes. When you finish, review and revise your notes. Add information that you remember. If helpful, consider rewriting your notes. Make the relationship between ideas clear and make important ideas stand out.

In about a week, your teacher will return your notes and give you a quiz on the information in the lecture. The purpose of this activity is to find out how well your notes help you to retain information.

POST-LECTURE READING AND DISCUSSION

Discuss the following in small groups.

1. Psychologists point out that there is a difference between "healthy striving" and "perfectionism." The following excerpt is from a publication by the University of Illinois at Urbana-Champaign's Counseling Center.

> Healthy goal setting and striving are quite different from the self-defeating process of perfectionism. Healthy strivers tend to set goals based on their own wants and desires rather than primarily in response to external expectations. Their goals are usually just one step beyond what they have already accomplished. In other words, their goals are realistic, internal, and potentially attainable. Healthy strivers take pleasure in the process of pursuing the task at hand rather than focusing only on the end result. When they experience disapproval or failure, their reactions are generally limited to specific situations rather than generalized to their entire self-worth.

Each sentence in the previous paragraph (except the first one) either implies or explicitly states a contrast between healthy goal setting and perfectionism. Write these differences in the following chart.

Healthy Strivers	Perfectionists
set goals based on their own wants & desires	set goals in response to external expectations

2. Do you think you are more of a healthy striver or a perfectionist? Use examples from your life to explain your answer.
3. The lecturer ends with a few suggestions for dealing with perfectionism. Read the longer list of suggestions that follows from the same University of Illinois at Urbana-Champaign Counseling Center publication. After reading, discuss your reactions to each suggestion. Do you think it is useful? Why or why not? Which suggestion, if any, would you most like to incorporate into your own life?

What to Do about Perfectionism

The first step in changing from perfectionistic attitudes to healthy striving is to realize that perfectionism is undesirable. Perfection is an illusion that is unattainable. The next step is to challenge the self-defeating thoughts and behaviors that fuel perfectionism. Some of the following strategies may help:

- Set realistic and reachable goals based on your own wants and needs and what you have accomplished in the past. This will enable you to achieve and also will lead to a greater sense of self-esteem.
- Set subsequent goals in a sequential manner. As you reach a goal, set your next goal one level beyond your present level of accomplishment.
- Experiment with your standards for success. Choose any activity and instead of aiming for 100%, try for 90%, 80% or even 60% success. This will help you to realize that the world does not end when you are not perfect.
- Focus on the process of doing an activity not just on the end result. Evaluate your success not only in terms of what you accomplished but also in terms of how much you enjoyed the task. Recognize that there can be value in the process of pursuing a goal.
- Use feelings of anxiety and depression as opportunities to ask yourself, "Have I set up impossible expectations for myself in this situation?"
- Confront the fears that may be behind your perfectionism by asking yourself, "What am I afraid of? What is the worst thing that could happen?"
- Recognize that many positive things can only be learned by making mistakes. When you make a mistake, ask, "What can I learn from this experience?" More specifically, think of a recent mistake you have made and list all the things you can learn from it.
- Avoid all-or-none thinking in relation to your goals. Learn to discriminate the tasks you want to give high priority to from those tasks that are less important to you. On less important tasks, choose to put forth less effort.

WRITING ACTIVITY

Write about one of the following topics.

1. Write an essay about an educational system that you know well. In what ways does this system encourage or discourage perfectionism? In what ways does it encourage or discourage healthy striving? Use information from the lecture and readings to support your ideas.

2. Write an essay about a culture that you know well. In what ways does this culture encourage or discourage perfectionism? In what ways does it encourage or discourage healthy striving? Use information from the lecture and readings to support your ideas.

3. Imagine that you are a school administrator. You want to educate parents about the dangers of pushing their children to become perfectionists. Write a letter to parents to persuade them that perfectionism will not help their children succeed. Use specific evidence from the lecture to support your ideas.

4. Write a response paper that presents your perspective on the information presented in this lecture unit. Synthesize, evaluate, and give your opinion on the information presented.

APPENDICES

LECTURE INDEX BY ORGANIZATIONAL PLAN

The organizational plan indicated occurs in either the entire lecture or a significant part of it.

Organizational Plan	Lecture Number and Title
Defining a Term	Lecture 6: How to Deal with Stress
	Lecture 7: Acid Rain
	Lecture 10: Pheromones
	Lecture 11: The Near Side of the Moon
	Lecture 15: Paging Robodoc: Robots in Medicine
	Lecture 17: Hall's Classification of Cultures
	Lecture 19: Perfectionism
Listing Subtopics	Lecture 1: The Process of Lecture Comprehension
	Lecture 2: Women and Work
	Lecture 3: American Attitudes toward Work
	Lecture 6: How to Deal with Stress
	Lecture 9: Amnesty International
	Lecture 13: Voter Turnout in the United States
	Lecture 19: Perfectionism
Describing a Causal Relationship	Lecture 7: Acid Rain
	Lecture 13: Voter Turnout in the United States
	Lecture 16: Earthquakes: Can They Be Predicted?
	Lecture 19: Perfectionism
Exemplifying a Topic	Lecture 8: Archaeological Dating Methods
	Lecture 10: Pheromones
	Lecture 13: Voter Turnout in the United States
	Lecture 14: How to Look at Art
	Lecture 15: Paging Robodoc: Robots in Medicine
	Lecture 17: Hall's Classification of Cultures
Describing a Process or Sequence of Events	Lecture 4: Milestones in Technology
	Lecture 5: Immigration to the United States
	Lecture 8: Archaeological Dating Methods
	Lecture 12: Drink Your Green Tea!
	Lecture 15: Paging Robodoc: Robots in Medicine

LECTURE INDEX BY SUBJECT MATTER

Subject Matter   **Lecture Number and Title**

*Social Sciences
and Humanities*

Anthropology   Lecture 8:   Archaeological Dating Methods
                      Lecture 18:   The Pyramids of Egypt: An Engineering Feat

Art   Lecture 14:   How to Look at Art

History   Lecture 15:   Immigration to the United States
                      Lecture 13:   Voter Turnout in the United States
                      Lecture 18:   The Pyramids of Egypt: An Engineering Feat

Linguistics   Lecture 1:   The Process of Lecture Comprehension

Political Science   Lecture 9:   Amnesty International
                      Lecture 13:   Voter Turnout in the United States

Psychology   Lecture 2:   Women and Work
                      Lecture 3:   American Attitudes toward Work
                      Lecture 6:   How to Deal with Stress
                      Lecture 17:   Hall's Classification of Cultures
                      Lecture 19:   Perfectionism

Sociology   Lecture 2:   Women and Work
                      Lecture 3:   American Attitudes toward Work
                      Lecture 5:   Immigration to the United States
                      Lecture 13:   Voter Turnout in the United States
                      Lecture 17:   Hall's Classification of Cultures

Sciences

Astronomy   Lecture 11:   The Near Side of the Moon

Biology   Lecture 10:   Pheromones
                      Lecture 12:   Drink Your Green Tea!
                      Lecture 15:   Paging Robodoc: Robots in Medicine

REWRITTEN NOTES FOR LECTURES

LECTURE 6 HOW TO DEAL WITH STRESS

STRESS — term originally used in physics

(to describe force betw. 2 touching masses)

— 40 years ago, Hans Selye adapted term

"the body's nonspecific response (incl. ↑ breathing,

heart rate, blood pressure, muscle tension) to any

demand placed on it, good or bad"

EUSTRESS (stress from good things)   e.g., tests

e.g., vacation, marriage

— Stress not hazardous in itself. Danger is in reaction to stress.

How to deal w/stress appropriately:

1. Learn to recognize signals of stress (before out of control)

e.g., irritability, insomnia, rapid weight loss/gain, ↑ smoking or drinking,

↑ "dumb" errors, phys. tension, tics, tightness of breath...

When see early signs, protect self! (withdraw fr. situation, reward self...)

2. Pay attention to body

exercise/nutrition can ↓ effect of stress on body & mind

— provides stress-free environment

3. Make plans & act when approp. (instead of worrying)

4. Learn to accept situations which are out of your control

(only ↑ stress if try to resist inevitable!)

5. Pace activities

break task into manageable parts

start fresh each day — recognize only 24 hrs./day!

Acid rain (AR): "any form of precipitation that contains high levels of acid

(partic. sulfuric acid & nitric acid)"

pH — scale for measuring acidity (7 = neutral)

pure rain = pH 5.6

lowest AR in U.S. = 1.4!

Causes of AR?

When N (nitrogen) and S (sulfur) go into atmosphere, they combine

w/ O (oxygen) and H (hydrogen)... form nitric acid (HNO_3) and

sulfuric acid (H_2SO_4)

Nitrogen Sources (in U.S.)

44.5% — transportation

50% — electric utilities (burning fuels for electric power)

5.5% — other

Sulfur Sources (in U.S.)

88% — electric util.

8.7% — other industrial sources (esp. coal burning power plants)

3.3% — transportation

Effects of AR?

On aquatic ecosystems: fish pops. ↓ or disappear

acid water kills fish or prevents reproduction

lakes look healthy but not true

On forests: certain trees die

Why? acidity strips protective surface

↓

trees vulnerable to water loss/disease

On architectural   buildings dissolving/crumbling

structures: billions $/yr. to replace

On health: no direct health effects

                      maybe indirect neg. effects (e.g., illness from

                         leaching of toxic metals in pipes)

Conclusions:

    AR $\uparrow$ w/industrialization

    (H_2O in glaciers from 200 yrs. ago (before Indust. Revolution) pH ~5

    What to do? Consider:

       shift to alternative nonpolluting energy

       create tech. to reduce release of S and N

         occurring worldwide

           new pollution-reduction laws (for cars, industry)

           agreements betw. countries to $\downarrow$ emissions

           problem: $\uparrow$ demand for power, transportation

AR — problem w/no natl. boundaries!

Archaeological Dating Methods:

Dendrochronology: tree-ring dating

                        one of oldest methods

    — measures tree rings which vary w/climatic changes

       (cross section of tree shows concentric rings)

          — pale ring — spring   — thin ring   — drought or cold spell

          — dark "   — winter   — thick "   — abundant water/sunlight

       — can measure back 1000s of years by matching rings w/known

          climatic events (don't need to count all)

Carbon-14 dating method — all living things contain radioactive C-14

                                isotopes which disintegrate at fixed

element w/same   rate when organism dies ($\frac{1}{2}$ every 5730 yrs.)

\# of protons but   "half-life"

diff. \# of neutrons   point at which half of element diminishes

    — scientists use geiger counter to measure C-14 signals fr. old material

      & compare this w/signals from living sample

        e.g., live sample: 75 disintegrations/min.

          old sample: 37.5 disintegrations/min.

        ∴ old sample = 5,730 yrs. old

Drawback of C-14 method:

    — requires large sample (up to 10 oz.)

    — destroys sample

Recent advances in C-14 dating: AMS: Accelerated Mass Spectrometry

    — focuses on measuring C-14 atoms rather than electric signals emitted

      by disintegration

    — advantages: smaller samples (1–2 mg.)

C-14 limited to 60,000 yrs.

There are other methods.

Most methods cross-checked for accuracy.

Amnesty International (AI)

— founded in 1961

— one of largest human rights org.

1998 — 1,100,000 members in 160 countries

— 1977 — Nobel Peace Prize

— 1978 — award by UN

Concerned only w/prisoners

— wants to release prisoners of conscience — "person detained for non-

— wants fair trials for all   violent expression of polit. or

— against torture   religious beliefs or for color,

— against death penalty   ethnicity, race, sex"

8 Principles of AI:

    1. limited mandate

        — does not work for all human rights — just concentrates on

          polit. prisoners, torture, execution

    2. focus on indiv. prisoner

        — wants specific details about indiv. not just general info.

        — AI adoption groups — groups of indiv. who work for indiv. prisoners

    3. action grounded in fact

        — wants reliable info. ∴ research

    4. based on member participation

        — AI believes indiv. makes difference

        — no human rights protection if left to govt. alone

        — AI built on indiv. effort

    5. moral suasion w/govt.

        — doesn't want conflict — seeks dialogue

        — doesn't want sanctions against govt.

        — wants feedback on reports from govt.

6. impartial in work

    — doesn't matter about politics, religion, ideology;

      AI works everywhere

    — won't compare/rank countries

7. independent in policy & finance

    — no links to state, polit. body, ideology, religion

    — only authority is membership

    — rules to protect independence

      — if have high post in govt., cannot have high post in AI

      — can't work for prisoners in own country

    — all finances from subscriptions

      — no gifts w/"strings"

      — no grants from govt. except relief

8. committed to intl. responsibility for human rights

    — human rights everyone's responsibility

    — not just own country's concern

Pheromones — "chemical substance released by organism into environment

to evoke response from other members of same species"

— detected by smell or taste

— widely used by animals — from 1 cell to higher primates

— Characteristics

— highly sensitive

— highly specific (each species responds only to own pheromones;

no effect on other species)

2 Types:

primer pher.   — causes phys. change in organism

— affects development & later behavior

e.g., queen bee prevents reproductive develop.

of ♀ worker bees

releaser pher. — produces rapid & reversible response

— immed. change

4 types (not mutually exclusive):

— alarm pher.

— warns of danger; response to threat

e.g., mouse releases odor; causes others to flee

— aggregation pher.

— calls members to 1 place for food, shelter, mating, etc.

e.g., honey bees — odor identifies colony; attracts

bees to colony

— sex pher.

— sexually arouses/attract species

e.g., mature female snails attract undifferentiated

snails (neither ♀ or ♂) & cause it to develop

into ♂

— terrestrial trail pher.

— navigational guide

e.g., ants follow trail to food

Pher. important to agriculture

Why?

— can control animal behavior to protect crops

— don't contain poison like traditional insecticides

— only affect 1 species; won't harm other species

Features of near side of moon — side perpetually turned to earth

<u>flat lowlands</u> — maria ("sea")   vs.   <u>highlands</u> — mountain ranges

— called "seas" but no liquid water   — lighter color & brighter than maria

— fairly smooth   — dominated by craters

— made of valleys & basins filled   — craters range in size

    w/molten lava   up to 150 mi.

    — basalt rock (igneous rock)   — highlands extend 100s of miles

— certain maria — areas of high   & up to 3.5+ mi. above maria

    concentration of mass (mascon)

    — mascon exert increased

      gravitational pull on

      spacecraft overhead

— circular maria (assoc. w/mascons)

    — up to 702 mi. diameter

— irreg. maria larger

Water on moon?

    — Until recently, scientists said no water on moon because moon lacked

      atmosphere (earth has liquid water because has atmosphere)

    — Now,.. questions!

      1998 lunar probe sent data showing possibility of ice crystals (in soil) in

      craters at lunar poles

    — if true — very important! ice could provide components for rocket fuel

    — issue needs more research

    — even if true... we don't have technol. to use ice yet!

Temperature on moon?

    — drastic changes in daily temp. — range from 215° F. → –285° F.

      Why?   no atmosphere (earth's atmos. is moderating blanket & limits

      diff. betw. day & night)

Light of near side of moon

— no twilight/dawn

— darkness/light — immediate when sun goes up or down (except for

small # of reflections from nearby peaks)

Why?   lack of atmosphere — nothing reflects light

(moon — 238,600 mi. away)

All tea — fr. camellia sinensis — evergreen, tropical, & semitrop. climates

3 ways to process tea leaves:

Green tea	Black tea	Oolong tea
"virgin" tea — least	more processing	semi-fermented
processed (~ 3 hr. process)	(needs fermentation)	green-brown
leaves steamed & heated	spread leaves in cool,	
to soften (& stop oxidation)	humid place	
↓	↓	
rolled (to remove	O₂ interacts w/leaves	
moisture)	(oxidation/fermentation)	
	causes leaves → black	
↓	↓	
dried	hot, dry air (15–25 min.)	
	stops oxidation	
World production: 20%	75%	4%

Green tea is good for you!

— Studies in China: G.T. reduces # of cancer esophagus

    — Studies (Japan)   ↓ lung cancer among people drinking GT

                ↓ stomach cancer

                ↓ skin tumors

                ↓ blood cholesterol

    — GT contains vit. C

       — av. 2 cups GT = 1 cup OJ

    — U.S. study — GT may help protect against cavities

Continuing research GT?

    — studied in NIH program w/40 other disease-fighting foods

       e.g., garlic, carrots

— scientists want to isolate & synthesize disease-fighting element

Why? preventative medicine

Problem? what element?

— focusing on "polyphenols"

GT — no known toxicity... won't hurt... may help

mild stimulant... GT < caffeine than coffee, black tea, soda

History of right to vote:

1. small group — property-owning white ♂

2. white ♂ w/o property

3. black ♂

4. 1920 — black & white ♀

long struggle to vote   BUT U.S. voter turnout low

— pres. election turnout

1960 — 64%

1988 — 50%

1992 — 55%

1996 — 49%

Causes of low voter turnout:

— not because of apathy.

2 reasons:

Institutional	Political
(registration & absentee ballot	(more important & more difficult
requirements — procedural	to change)
requirements)	— feel voting not worth trouble
— forget to register	— feel no choice betw. candidates
— moved; didn't reg.	or parties
— think reg. takes time	— mistrust politicians
— inconvenient reg. hrs.	— feel politicians apathetic
— early reg. deadlines	about them

Poll — asked why people didn't vote

38% — didn't register (reason? apathy? institutional? political?)

14% — polit. reasons (e.g., didn't like candidate)

18% — institutional reasons (e.g., sick, new resident, etc.)

10% — not interested in politics

10% — no reason

10% — not U.S. citizen or other reasons

Voter/Nonvoter characteristics

    — as education ↑ voting ↑ regardless of race/ethnicity

    — as income & career status ↑ voting ↑

    — as age ↑ voting ↑ (until ~ 70)

        — ages 18-24 and 70+ — poor voting records

    — whites vote > blacks > Hispanics

    — ♀ vote slightly > ♂

TREND — poor, uneducated, & minorities underrepresented in voting.

    — not accidental — part of polit. and psych. environment that

    discourages polit. activity of minorities (Burns et al.)

Picture not so bleak — why?

    — Americans have > elections than other countries

    — Americans have right not to vote; no one forced

Maybe w/ ↑ ♀ and minorities in politics, ↓ disillusionment

Directed Looking

— way to <u>look</u> at art

— involves examining works directly (not reading about work or

studying history)

Components of "directed looking" approach: 5 categories of observation

(in real life, categories overlap)

1. Observing physical properties

e.g., size? mediums? how mediums applied? textures? 2-D or 3-D?

2. Exploring subject matter — need to examine representative and

abstract

— representative (still life, portrait, etc.)

— sometimes subject matter more than just objects

— e.g., Van Gogh's <u>Hospital Corridor</u>

— represents hall

— subject matter not hall... maybe fear? confusion?

— abstract

e.g., Kline — <u>Painting #2</u> — maybe about growth? progress?

3. Observing illusionary properties — how artist makes us believe something

impossible (e.g., 3-D on 2-D paper, distance)

— create 3-D through shading, highlighting

(Callahan photo, no shading ∴ seems "flat")

— techniques for creating illusion of distance?

— smaller seems farther (e.g., door in Van Gogh's <u>Hospital</u>)

— out of focus seems farther

4. Observing formal elements (line, color, shape, composition)

how line (explicit & implied), color, shape arranged

how space & shapes interact

focal points

— e.g., lines — heavy? light? choppy?

    — explicit lines? e.g., Hopper (<u>Early Sunday Morning</u>)

    — implied lines? e.g., Lange (<u>Migrant Mother</u>) — implied diagonal up

                                            arm to face

    — shapes? touching? overlapping?

        — e.g., Hopper (full of rectangles, squares — represent regularity

        of life?)

    — colors? realistic? effects?

        — e.g., Hopper painting — bright yellow shades stand out

        against dark

5. Observing viewer perspective — where artist positions viewer

    — e.g., looking at object from below? above? equal level? from far? near?

        — Degas' <u>Orchestra of Opera</u> — viewer looks up at stage

Robot: word fr. Czech "forced labor"

Robot Industries Assoc. definition: "a reprogrammable, multifunctional,

manipulator designed to move material, parts, tools, or specialized devices

through variable programmed motions to perform a variety of tasks"

    "reprogrammable" — can get new instructions

    "multifunctional" — can perform variety of tasks

How robots work:

    — microprocessor is "brain"

    — most robots have single hand & arm (w/5 or 6 joints)

    "end effector" (sometimes w/2 "fingers," sometimes just tools)

Robots use in hospitals: e.g., Robodoc

    — first generation robot tech. in hospitals

    — more precise & steady than humans

    — esp. useful in hip replacement

        Why?   Surgery is physically laborious

                high # of this surgery

in past — surgeons manually carved cavity & bore holes in thighbone

        — resulted in rough fit for implant

        — used cement to hold implant but cement lost grip

        (after 5–10 yrs) & many needed surgery again

    w/Robodoc — computer image finds exact size of cavity for implant

        — Robodoc makes hole; implant fits exactly

Process of hip replacement surgery w/Robodoc (~ 90 min.)

    — surgeon takes CT scan of femur

    — " " transfers image to computer

    — " " views image & chooses implant (from computer memory)

    — " " stores info. in computer

    — in operating room, surgeon exposes femur

— computer gives robot instructions about cavity & implant

— Robodoc drills cavity

— after ~ 20 min., surgeon fits implant & completes surgery

Some resistance to robots:

— fear robots will replace surgeons

— fear robots will "go crazy"

developers emphasize robots ASSIST surgeons, not replace

+ lots of safety controls

Earthquakes (EQ) — ~ 30,000 + annually (most minor)

    ~ 75 significant (many in unpopulated areas)

    <u>EQ — "the vibration of the Earth produced by the rapid release of energy"</u>

EQ Cause:

    — some caused by atomic explosions or volcanic eruption but infrequent

    — most caused by slippage along Earth's crust

    — releases energy which radiates from source in waves (like stone dropped in pond)

    — Plate tectonics theory: large slabs of Earth's crust — in continual slow motion

        — tectonic forces deform rock on both sides of fault (break in rock)

        — rocks bend and store energy (like bending wooden stick)

        — slippage occurs at weakest point spreading along fault

            — releases strain (like stick breaking)

        — rock returns (like stretched rubber band) to original shape ("elastic rebound") — these vibrations are EQ

EQ Prediction:

    — most research in EQ affected countries

        e.g., Japan, U.S., China, Russia

    <u>2 types of EQ Prediction Research</u>

<u>Short-Range Prediction</u>	<u>Long-Range Prediction</u>
— based on phenomena preceding EQ	— based on premise that EQs are repetitive/cyclical
— changes in animal behavior	
— changes in seismic activity	— scientists look for patterns
e.g., quiet followed by lot of activity	e.g., CA: seismologists said EQ occur every 22 yrs... next in 1988 but still waiting!
— changes in ground water levels near faults	— so far not useful

          — changes in electric currents or

            radio waves

          — emission of gas (e.g., radon)

   1 success: China 1975 — evacuated

     3 mil. people before major EQ

     But scientists skeptical (this area

     never had EQs, and suddenly had

     tremors) maybe just good guess

     (1 yr. later — major EQ not predicted)

Almost all seismologists agree — short-term EQ prediction difficult, if not

    impossible

Some have hope for long-term prediction

Edward Hall — anthropologist — works w/Am. Indian

— studies relation betw. cultures not just culture

— believes diff. cultures have diff. assumptions about time, space, relations

— classifies culture on continuum — high/low context

HALL'S CLASSIFICATION

High-Context	Low-Context
context of message/action (what is happening around message) carries more meaning than message itself	message seen as separate w/meaning in itself; more attention to message than context

	High-Context	Low-Context
Interpersonal Relationships	dependence on shared info. re: event	rely on legal bonds not social bonds
	e.g., less legal paperwork	e.g., contract > important
	e.g., person's word is bond	than spoken word
	e.g., depend on power of networks > indiv.	
	e.g., loan $ because of family NOT indiv.	
	depend on social not legal restraints	depend on law to control behavior
	e.g., don't break law because of what people think not fear of punishment	
	strong feeling of respons. for group	responsibility passed as
	e.g., in org. if something wrong,	far down as poss.
	top person takes blame	("pass the buck")

Personal Space	more physical closeness	concept of "personal space"
	e.g., stand closer, touch a lot	(people feel violated if this space is invaded)
		e.g., stand farther, touch less
	less respect for privacy	more respect & desire for privacy
	awareness of body language	less aware of body language
Time	polychronic attitude	monochronic attitude
	— everything has "own" time	— everything follows same time
	∴ no one standard of time	
	— punctuality not important	— punctuality important
	— clock time not important	— see time as commodity ("time is $")
Advantage	provides social security through social bonds & tradition	more indiv. independence allows greater differences & creativity
Disadvantages	change comes slowly	less commitment to system;
	rigid structure may bind people	less human trust

Cultures on the continuum (ex. from Hall)

Low-context									High-context
German-Swiss	German	Scandinavian	U.S.	French	English	Italian	Spanish	Greek	Arab

* All people unaware of assumptions about reality; unconsciously learn about time, space, etc.

* "mind" is really internalized culture

* important to consider this in multicultural education

NOTES